Education for Spiritual Growth traces out the common thread of meditation that links these various traditions and shows how it relates to the fully developed inner life. Cully helps readers discern their own reasons for seeking spiritual growth; she stresses the importance of discerning between objectivity and subjectivity—knowing the difference between a retreat ending in privatism and a retreat that brings one back into the world renewed. Clarifying insights into theological, psychological, social, and educational implications of the inner quest are presented, as are the ways we can learn from one another along the spiritual way and the important role played by the larger believing community.

In sum, *Education for Spiritual Growth* compellingly proves the author's contention that "the spiritual life can be nurtured in individuals at each age level through a knowledge of the developmental aspects of life, an understanding of the nature of the Christian community, and the influence of worship in its many forms. Through long-understood methods, people can be taught how to deepen their relationship to God through silence, interaction with an individual who is a spiritual friend, and the support of a small group. Spiritual growth comes through an interrelationship between nurture and education, an understanding of the relationship of human beings within the created world, an awareness of God as both transcendent and immanent, and an internalization of meanings to be found in the Cross, central to new life in the Spirit."

Iris V. Cully, widely recognized as a leading authority in the field of religious education, is the author of nine previous books, including *Christian Child Development.* Dr. Cully, an Episcopalian, was the first woman appointed to the faculty of Yale Divinity School, a distinction repeated in 1976 at Lexington Theological Seminary, Kentucky, where she is now professor of religious education.

EDUCATION FOR SPIRITUAL GROWTH

Education for Spiritual Growth

IRIS V. CULLY

1817

Harper & Row, Publishers, San Francisco
Cambridge, Hagerstown, New York, Philadelphia
London, Mexico City, São Paulo, Sydney

Designer: Jim Mennick

Library of Congress Cataloging in Publication Data

Cully, Iris V.
   EDUCATION FOR SPIRITUAL GROWTH.

   Includes index.
   1. Spiritual life. I. Title.
   BV4501.2.C85   1984   248.4   83-48464
   ISBN 0-06-061655-5

---

85   86   87   88   10   9   8   7   6   5   4   3   2

To
The Society of the Companions of the Holy Cross
Who for a Century
Have Both Practiced and Shared the Spiritual Life

Contents

Preface

Deepening the spiritual life has become important to people. Living in a tension-filled world, they want release from anxiety. Theirs is a quest for inner peace. During the 1960s people began to seek such peace through disciplined meditative techniques derived from Asian religions. They seemed unaware that these had long been a part of their own Christian past. Most Protestant groups have not recognized this dimension of Christian history. An emphasis on Christian living as activity had made it unlikely that people would be encouraged in contemplation. In recent times, only in the congregational worship of the Society of Friends, and in the training provided in Roman Catholic seminaries, monasteries, and convents, has a disciplined spirituality been taught and practiced. At one time, Frank Buchman's Moral Rearmament movement was popular among some groups. Part of this program was the daily family gathering to listen to God.

The resurgence of interest in the long tradition of Christian spirituality seems for many to be a discovery. To answer the need, new editions of the classical writings in spirituality from many traditions are being published. There is a plethora of new books under the heading of "spirituality and . . ." Renewal movements draw many people to retreats and conferences for the examination of their faith and the deepening of their commitment. Prayer groups become important to parishes.

All these contribute to the spiritual life, but they are not quick roads to inner peace. The spiritual life must be cultivated. Cultivation is a process of nurture and education. Spirituality is never a product. It is a process evidenced in a lifestyle. The purpose of this book is to help people learn about and nurture spiritual growth in their own lives. It is also to help them become teachers who can nurture others into spiritual development.

Believers are on pilgrimage, as people of the biblical faith have always seen life as pilgrimage. Beginners are helped on the way by the more experienced who share their faith. This book is designed to help individuals in their quest.

Groups that form for the purpose of sharing spiritual experience and deepening their relationship to God through time spent together are looking for ways to accomplish this purpose. This book is written with them in mind also.

A new phenomenon is the interest in structured classes, through which a course may be designed to help people understand and develop the spiritual life. Such classes are being formed in parishes, colleges, and theological seminaries. This book is planned for their use, too.

The design begins with a chapter that explores aspects of the quest for serenity. The *process* of spiritual growth is examined. Two chapters give biblical and historical background and the experience of other religious traditions. Readers are next invited to examine their reason for seeking spiritual resources: is it a retreat from life, or a strengthening for life? Theological, biblical, and psychological roots are then explored.

Each chapter concludes with the educational implications of the theme. The last three chapters are specifically concerned with aspects of nurture, methods for spiritual development, and the interaction of nurture and education.

Appreciation goes to my husband, Kendig Brubaker Cully, who continues to reinforce my work, and takes time for painstaking editing. Appreciation goes also to Mary L. Cole and Nan G. McSwain, whose elegantly typed drafts made revision almost a pleasure. Finally, research was made easier through the resources of the Lexington Theological Seminary Library and the helpfulness of the librarian, Roscoe M. Pierson, and the staff.

1. Hearts That Are Restless

The quest for serenity is a phenomenon of the times. The yearning for peace within restless hearts has spawned numerous techniques for achieving this goal. From every avenue of life, people are offering their testimonies that a new-found peace has allayed anxiety, increased efficiency, and made their days more worthwhile. Week by week, the guests on the Reverend Robert Schuller's televised church service witness to how God has changed their lives. Evangelists urge change of heart. Counselors urge change of mind. Religious communities urge change of lifestyle.

The trend was highlighted by a report from the *New York Times* religion editor, Kenneth A. Briggs, in an article entitled "Faith Inspires These Actors' Efforts." He states that meditative practices have long been used among performers to reduce stress, while writers and composers have found them to be aids to concentration that also freed the imagination. A group of players from the popular musical *Ain't Misbehavin'* were accustomed to gathering in a lounge at the theater between afternoon and evening performances for prayer and meditation. Before performances the cast gathered quietly onstage for an informal moment of meditation.[1]

The quest is not new. Manuals on spirituality have been written for hundreds of years. Practices of spirituality have been handed down through cultures for generations. About forty years ago there were a trio of books that stayed on best seller lists for weeks and even years. *Peace of Mind* was written by Joshua Loth Liebman, a well-known rabbi living in the Boston area; *Peace of Soul* by a priest of radio fame, Fulton J. Sheen;

and *The Power of Positive Thinking* by a perennially popular New York minister, Norman Vincent Peale.[2] These books answered the needs of a people torn by war and yearning for peace in the world, peace in their land, freedom from anxiety in their personal and family lives; in short, a return to normalcy as they understood it.

The world seems to be in such a period again. One could analyze the external factors, but these do not get at the crux of the matter. The yearning itself proclaims the fact that people know they must find peace *in spite of* the surrounding threats in life, and that they must somehow find it within themselves. Long ago, St. Augustine of Hippo wrote in his autobiographical work, the *Confessions*, "Thou hast made us for thyself; and our hearts are restless until they find their rest in thee." Today, millions echo those words. Many of them do not know where or in whom they will find their rest, but with eager yearning they pursue the search.

Escape from Anxiety

The quest for serenity begins with a negative impulse. People do not at first seek positive steps to achieve peace. Rather they hope to eliminate the causes that prevent them from having peace. Serenity is a lovely word. It brings images of a calm that is beyond tumult, a rest beyond turbulence. Serenity seems divine. Peace is a part of serenity—a quietude of heart, mind, and soul. Serenity is a total attitude of being, an equilibrium maintained through all vicissitudes of life. No wonder people are more likely to think about eliminating those factors in life that prevent the development of serenity rather than finding ways to attain peace.

We want to be freed from anxiety. Anxiety is not concern. Concern is a feeling toward other people and events that keeps us human. Anxiety may be of the type that psychologists label "free-floating"—a vague unrest that seemingly has no cause. Anxiety may be what the philosophers know as a pervasive sense that the world is doomed, that the perfection for which humans have strived is not attainable. It may be a restless yearning toward that which can never be.

But anxiety can also have a practical base. People are anxious about having sufficiency in material things so that they can live with some sense of decency and, beyond that, comfort. Because money is the basis for buying necessities such as food, clothing, housing, and health care—and because work is the source for obtaining money, employment or lack of it becomes a major element in anxiety. Sometimes, finding and keeping any form of work may bring anxiety. In other situations, anxiety concerns the kind and quality of work. Is the work equal to my ability? Is it enhancing my life and that of my family? Is it ethical? Is it giving stability to the community? Is it helping the world community, socially and economically? In the answers to one or more of these questions lies the sense of personal fulfillment in work.

Although work is the source of income for some, as pensions or investments may be for others, work alone does not satisfy anxiety concerning material possessions. Some people are never satisfied. They seek peace in the multitude of objects they possess. A well-appointed house, a well-filled clothes closet—these surely will bring a feeling of well-being, they think. For others, it is the quality of possessions: to have the newest or most popular objects, to have the most perfect collection of eighteenth-century glass, to own a famous painting that has just been placed on the market, to be among the best-dressed men or women in one's social set.

Having sufficient possessions is a subtle goal that may even include house or neighborhood, the club in which one holds membership, or the schools that children attend. This is a far cry from the intent of that petition voiced daily by Christians everywhere, "Give us this day our daily bread." As every yearning beyond that need becomes a gnawing desire, the hope of serenity evaporates. To enjoy luxuries beyond daily bread, when such are available, may be a good response to the wealth provided by God in creation. To make them the focus for life goals is to forfeit all hope of serenity.

Despite the abundance of creation, millions of people are hungry every day, and the main reason for high child mortality rates in some areas of the world is malnutrition. There are whole countries where masses of the population are unemployed or underemployed, and few, if any, countries where all who need or want jobs have them. The systems which have developed—or simply have been allowed to grow—prevent the achievement of serenity among millions.

Another cause of anxiety concerns the sense of well-being, a simple acceptance of the self. People set up some standard of moral achievement, and then judge themselves unworthy because they are not perfect. Even efforts at loving others are doomed, for love is expressed, not achieved. There is restlessness where there could be peace because people are unwilling to be the person God intended them to be. Much of this anxiety arises from internalizing standards other people have set: parents, first—so long ago that adults scarcely realize the source of their own disquiet about themselves. Expectations of community, social group, or church keep a person looking outside for norms rather than within. It is an irony that church communities, supposedly havens of peace, frequently generate anxiety through their expectations of what it means to live as a Christian. Indeed, one technique of evangelism is to generate anxiety in order to lead a person through guilt to remorse, repentance, and the concluding peace of regeneration. Some years ago, a discerning writer for children penned a poem that affirms this sense of self:

> I am glad I'm who I am
> I like to be myself
> Even when I do the wrong thing
> I know I am the right person.[3]

There is a consistency in personhood that needs to be discovered and respected. People indeed do wrong things, but by seeing actions in relation to authentic being, they can change the actions to direct the best of their own being toward other people. In this way lies serenity.

Only after a person has achieved this sure sense of personhood is it possible to engage in relationships that enhance both one's personal being and that of others.[4] There can be no serenity while a person is anxious about what others think. This factor pushes a person's concern beyond the self in a negative way. The real emphasis is not on the other but on the self. Such a person is tied down by anxiety. Relationships encompass a wide area of life: family, neighbors, church, community, and work. How could anyone live up to the potentially diverse expectations of so many people? Self-acceptance includes acceptance of the fact that some people will not agree with who you are, how you act, or what you think. This poses a situation threatening to the self, but one who has serenity accepts the possibility.

Another source of anxiety arises from uncertainties about one's work. Consider the mother or father with parenting goals that are beyond human achievement, since children are *themselves*, too, and will not always meet expectations. Or the spouse who has an ideal for marriage—and who may even be prodded by the other partner toward a self-image that is not authentic. Or a church member who believes there is only one way of being a Christian and pursues this illusion, though it means forfeiting the faith that comes from grace alone. Or the homemaker who tries to mold a whole family into maintaining an environment that looks like a photo from a magazine. Or a worker who returns home each day exhausted from the effort to be better, more perfect, more fully achieving. These are not pathways to serenity.

Many are also anxious about the future. Perhaps most persons fall into this category at some time, and some are always filled with foreboding as they contemplate what lies ahead. The check-out counter at the supermarket sells magazines addressed to this source of anxiety. Reading about predictions of the future helps some people feel that they have a handle on the unknown. These events may not happen, but readers have been forewarned. They have some idea what to expect. The problem is that such persons continue to look for prognostications. Anxiety is never allayed. Each tomorrow is a new future, and becomes another cause for anxiety. People may seek a solution in fantasy or in learned treatises. Some turn to astrologers, whose ancient ways still bring hope. Others turn to scholars, whose researches and computer-based data bring comfort. Whether through magazines (popular or learned), books (romances or research), or television (fantasy or fact), people search the media to fill their need for inner peace.

In a nuclear age, a form of global anxiety becomes almost overwhelming. People want to know the worst possible scenario, so that they can hope for something better. The anxiety in the threat of nuclear destruction, writes Jonathan Schell, is not simply in what can happen to our persons and possessions, but in the possibility that there will be no human future.[5] This is more than human imagining can bear to contemplate. Who can promise serenity in such a time as this?

Escape from Hostility

The quest for serenity also involves freedom from feelings of hostility. Anger and peace are antithetical. They exist within the same person only as a constant source of turmoil and unrest. Yet people bristle with hostility. "Life is not treating me fairly," they say.[6] They are angry at God—who for religious people has been thought to be the very source of serenity. They are angry at all the people who might be causing them to feel they are treated unfairly. They are, whether they know this or not, angry at themselves. As long as they say, "Why has this happened to *me?*" there will never be peace. They assume that for some special reason, life should be all sunshine for them. They want to believe that they are somehow better (whatever that means) than other people who also suffer. "Others deserve this; I do not."

If anger is not the answer, neither is resignation, because resignation may include suppressed anger. The only source of peace lies in an acceptance that includes awareness of the totality of suffering in the world: suffering that people bring on themselves deliberately or by accident; suffering that is caused by other people or events beyond personal control; suffering that comes through natural disasters. The meaning of suffering may not be found in the suffering itself, but in an acceptance of what it means to be fully human and to participate in the pain of the world—which includes the pain of God, whom Christians see as suffering through the passion of their Lord, Jesus Christ.

Hostility toward life finds still another focus in a culture that is oriented toward some definition of progress. For many people progress includes rising to the top in their work. Promotions bring not only status, money, and some security. They also bring a sense of achievement and self-worth. The self-image is frequently tied up with achievement, and the sense of failure arising from lack of tangible signs of success may lead a person to protect the self by the arousal of hostility toward those in authority, fellow workers, family, and society. "If the boss did not have favorites," "If my spouse were more supportive," "If another political party were in power"—these and other "ifs" ease personal feelings of inadequacy. But they do not bring peace; they do not lead to the cultivation of serenity.

A person's hostility may be sensed by those who are closest. Divorce usually signals mutual hostility between husband and wife. Runaway and delinquent young people are acting out hostility toward families, schools, and communities. Alcoholism and other forms of drug addiction dramatize the desperation of persons trying to still the pangs of anxiety and hostility. Strange ways of seeking peace, we may think, but the fact is that people reach for panaceas when they have no hope for cures. They believe that no one loves them: neither spouse, parents, children, nor friends. This idea may be only in their imaginations, but illusions are real to those who believe in them. A feeling of worthlessness causes people to be hostile. This may be a negative way of self-defense, but it is the only one some people know. They need a way out.

Hostility may arise in a person from resentment of what is perceived as unrealistic expectations by other people. An inner voice says, "Your wife wants you to be this," "Your father expects this from you," "As an elder in the church you should act this way," "As a worker in the company this is how you should present our image." Some people try to absorb such expectations, however inimical to the self. Others are able to ask themselves how they can become enriched through their associations and relationships. All people are shaped by the environment and influenced by the people among whom they live and work. Some, unsure of themselves, feel pulled in many directions, and develop a hostility that precludes self-enhancement. Others are able to decide for themselves what they will accept in terms of society's demands. These can develop that elusive quality called serenity.

The Quest for Power

Some people are restless, not because they seek a peace that will free them from anxiety or hostility, but because they seek power. They expect power to become the basis for peace. When you have reached the top, achieved position, money, and influence, surely this will bring fulfillment, and fulfillment will bring serenity.

Or will it? More likely, the quest for power is a divergent goal from that of achieving peace. Power is, in the root sense, *dynamic*, ever restless. It may be at the opposite pole of existence from peace. There is a stasis to peace. Some might view it as an absence of conflict; others as a rest from activity. Neither, however, is an accurate description. To have peace an individual must first resolve conflict in the self and come to terms in a positive way with whatever conflict may lie in a situation.

Power may also be the other side of the coin. Certainly there is a quiet power in serenity. This sort of power brings an image of the ocean that may, in clear weather, show gentle waves on top while surging with power underneath. This sort of power is known only to those who are still long enough to hear what God has to say, as the prophet Elijah so long ago learned. There are many kinds of power.

To have power, then, does not necessarily mean to dominate. To the religious person, to have dominion or power always means to hold this authority as a gift from God to be used for God's purposes. The person who has achieved power over other persons is in a dangerous situation. There is always room at the top because people are always falling from or being dislodged from the top. Hence, to have power is to be vulnerable.

There is, however, a legitimate yearning for earthly power. People need a sense of achievement. The psychologist Erik Erikson long ago pointed out that children from the ages of six to twelve need to learn how to develop skills to a degree that gives them a feeling of competency.[7] His insight was amplified by Jerome Bruner, who spearheaded a whole movement toward new forms of cognitive learning in the 1960s.[8] Adults who have had an opportunity to achieve competency in childhood continue to find satisfaction in achievement. They want to become more skilled as mechanics, more competent as engineers, more alert as executives, more creative as homemakers. When they have achieved their own full potential, they will feel powerful. But in a culture that makes room for only one person "at the top," where even the ordering of words suggests grading and ranking, numbers of people may become highly competent but still feel restless. They ought to feel that they have done well, but the sense of power is lacking. They can only feel successful if someone else is less successful.

This attitude is self-defeating. Of all the creative, contributing people in the world today, only a few have wide name recognition and fewer still are recognized by name and face. Given copies of the well-known *Time* magazine January covers for the past thirty years, without names attached to faces, how many people would recognize the man or woman of the year? Achievement can only bring satisfaction when it is an expression of personal fulfillment.

Another form of power comes from the sense of having overcome difficulty, disaster, or failure. A person who experiences this feels "on top" in a different way; that is, on top of a threatening situation. Life can seem like an uphill climb. For some people, it is similar to the task of rolling a boulder up the mountain, only to have it fall back each time, as in the ancient legend of Sisyphus. One never achieves the summit. For others it is like the situation of a person who climbs one mountain, only to look across a broad valley to the next mountain, which then becomes the goal: thus on and on. These are the restless ones for whom no achievement brings either satisfaction, power, or peace.

Other people find achievement in each obstacle overcome. They do not have to wait until the completion of their course of study, but only the completion of one required assignment. They do not have to wait until the whole house is built, but only to see each step successfully accomplished. The improvement of a skill that leads to making an improved product gives satisfaction.

Some people are devastated by one failure. Others assume that the road to success is littered with failures. Stories about people in business tell of fortunes lost and regained three times over, of companies that have failed and then been reorganized. Writers tell of a book rejected numerous times, then accepted and a best seller. Inventors work for years to perfect a product that will not only be patented but marketed. Scientists pursue hypotheses until a breakthrough heralds a new realm of knowledge. These people look on failure as one avenue of learning.

They can accept it, and in acceptance is their peace.

To overcome disaster may be the most difficult task. It raises the earlier question of "why did this happen to me?" Some people do not recover; they are destroyed. Others acquiesce and never regain the kind of life they had earlier. Others accept the face of disaster and are able to build a future on the slimmest of possibilities. Life and selfhood have meaning. There is for these people a possibility of serenity that comes through the devastations of life. They have a long-term view that has seen the purposes of God working *through* events as well as *in spite* of events. This is their form of achieving power, and through it serenity.

Success is made bitter for some people because of its transitory nature. People retire, grow old, cease to be productive, or die. The final form of power is to be remembered. The Bible is a book of remembering. The Hebrew people were taught to remember and to tell their children how God brought them out of bondage into freedom. In a similar way, people with power wish that they could be remembered in history. Most people know that this will not happen. Sufficient to have been listed in the annals of their school, church, or community. They will hope to be named to their great grandchildren. They hardly know their own ancestors beyond the third generation. To be remembered is to have power over the future—over students who have to memorize names, dates, and achievements, over workers whose tasks are built on a foundation you laid. And yet—how many Nobel Prize winners can you name—even in a field you know? How many presidents of the United States can you recall? There finally comes the realization that to be remembered is an achievement for the few. The restlessness that results from seeking power will not be quieted by yearnings toward fame. The quest for power is a road of endless struggle. To some the struggle is a necessary part of life. Others develop a vague feeling that something has been missed, that without some degree of serenity, the struggle has not led anywhere.

The Quest for Security

Another reason for restless hearts is the quest for security. The more unstable one's world seems to be, the more intense is the yearning for security. The church, or any other religious community, has been a final refuge and source of security. For this reason it tilts toward the conservative. An important role of the church is to preserve customs and conserve values. People want to know with some certainty who God is, how God acts, and how they are supposed to live. They seek purpose in their lives and in the world. "Change and decay in all around we see; help of the helpless O abide with me," writes the hymnodist contemplating the end of life.

But the church is part of society. It is composed of people with certain beliefs and commitments. The church also changes, however glacially, in the estimate of its critics. The perception of these changes in any area of its life convinces adherents that a final source of security has been removed. The church represents God. If the church does not mirror God, and cannot give security, one must look elsewhere.

One place where people look is within themselves. The only person you can trust is yourself, they will affirm. "Look Out for Number One" was a slogan encapsulated in a popular book. Some refer to this phenomenon as privatization. Others call it self-centeredness. According to the viewpoint, this process may be either good or bad. To trust oneself is to have a sure sense of one's being, a positive self-image that cannot be easily damaged by outside assault. This requires an integrity and authenticity that many dream of having but not everyone achieves. Alternatively a person may become insulated from other lives.

Thus people could become cut off from a source of peace through this kind of self-centeredness. Far from leading to a solution, they are part of their own problem. To depend entirely on the self becomes a source of insecurity. Such an attitude removes a person from the possibilities of self-enhancement through relationships with other people. This is limiting, if not self-defeating.

Can you really trust yourself? Of course! You have to be able to trust yourself before you can trust anyone else. Erik Erikson again speaks to human development when he pinpoints the development of basic trust in the under-two child as essential to healthy personality development. The antithesis is mistrust, which develops when a lack of secure nurturing makes impossible the development of trust. He continues by saying that such trust in another human being is also the basis for the religious person's trust in God. Those who think it possible to live without religious faith will need to find it elsewhere in human relationships.[9]

The child develops trust in the self by being surrounded by one or more persons who themselves have sufficient trust in life to be able to love and nurture the infant generously. The trust given and received at the very beginning of life is the basis on which mature trust develops. The tragedy of those who are abandoned, alienated, or cast out is that they no longer have anyone in whom they can trust.

Restlessness drives these people to seek other objects in which to place their trust. The key to security may be sought in education and the development of competencies; in achievement, power, money, or social status. The fulfillment of such objectives may bring pleasure and pride. It may quell anxiety and uncertainty. Achievement brings its own exhilaration and even a certain contentment.

But these do not still the restless search for serenity. The spiritual quest can be entered at any level of life and in any condition of life. It invites the powerful and the powerless, the competent and the incompetent, the secure and the insecure, the hostile and the benevolent, the anxious, and those who have found some peace.

Education for Spirituality and Need Fulfillment

A mature spirituality is home for the restless heart. Human beings, made in the image of their creator God, seek a depth of relationship with God that may reach a form of union. Saints whose lives have been aflame with devotion attest to this. But such spirituality does not come naturally to anyone, although the yearning for a deeper spiritual awareness is natural. Just as human relationships mature through the years when carefully cultivated, so the relationship to God, which we call the spiritual life, can only be developed slowly. It is an educative process. God is the teacher. Spiritual guides who have gone farther along the path are assistants. All education is a process, and education in the spiritual life continues throughout life.

The Christian year through which we move as the people of God can be a prototype for spiritual development. The first note is the Advent of one expectation—an eager yearning that God may be revealed, and that the believer may be overcome by grace and glory. Searching in the scriptures tells of the promise, warns of the waiting. "Get you up to a high mountain. O Zion, herald of good tidings." The beginning of the Christian year is like the beginning of the spiritual journey.

The expectation is fulfilled in a burst of light and song. Joy overwhelms with the announcement that the One who is promised has come. The feast of the Nativity is our time of spiritual enlightenment. "Let us go now unto Bethlehem," we say with the shepherds. The star goes before us as it did before the visitors from a distant land. And what do we see when we arrive? The quiet simplicity of the stable, the Holy One among the animals, in the care of simple parents. Is this the nature of spiritual reality? Mary did not assume anything; she "kept all these things and pondered them in her heart." Contemplation and meditation are means for the spiritual life even in the moment of its most wondrous revelation.

The revelation of God is not something that can be kept to

oneself. It is a gift to be shared. This is the meaning of Epiphany: the showing forth of the Lord. As the shepherds returned to their work, glorifying God, so the Magi, after presenting gifts to the incarnate One, returned to their own country. The gospels record the showing forth: the child in the temple, the baptism in Jordan, the sign of water changed into wine, the preaching from the mount. The spiritual life is deepened through contemplation of these events. Moreover, the Epiphany is to the whole world, as the Book of Acts proclaims: to Antioch, the province of Asia, across the sea to Greece, and to Rome.

Caught up into the heady atmosphere of such august appearings, the believer is as unprepared as was Peter for a turning toward Jerusalem. It is good to be on the mountain, to witness healings, to sit rapt before the teacher, to receive promise of the keys to the kingdom. But to leave comfortable Galilee for threatening Jerusalem, seat of both temporal and spiritual power? Be that far from you, Lord, and we don't want to go either. Lent begins with a successful assault on temptation and ends with an unsuccessful plea to avoid the Cross. The spiritual journey proceeds on a rocky road, filled with suffering. It is not what some seekers after the beatific vision expect. It is an unlikely avenue to self-fulfillment. With every Lent that comes in a lifetime, the meaning of the word serenity is tested.

But the initiated, those who have been baptized into the Lord Jesus Christ, know already that they are baptized into his death in order that they may be participants in his resurrection. Every Calvary in life is excruciatingly painful, but each is endurable because of the certainty of Easter. This, like Epiphany, is a season of fulfillment. The Lord appears in everyday life: to a couple inviting him for supper, to friends gathered in the upper room they had earlier shared with him, to fishermen bringing to shore a night's catch. Not angel songs and gifts of Magi this time. The spiritual life is more advanced. The presence of the Holy One can be discerned in every area of life.

Entrance into the resurrected life leads to a new burst of

energy: the descent of the Holy Spirit among the disciples. God comes with power that energizes every life touched by the Spirit. Here is power to live, to witness, and to die. The long season of the Holy Spirit, Pentecost, is half a year—or at least half a lifetime. The appearance will be in turn comforting or disturbing, but God is never absent. Restless hearts have found their rest at last.

What happens as people begin to develop the spiritual life? To begin with, they are helped to answer questions about the self and others. When they ask, "Who am I?" it is not in a restless search, but in order to know more fully what it means to be a child of God who has created and redeemed us. The spirit-filled life is that of an authentic self that does not need to live in anxiety or hostility, nor to seek affirmation through various forms of human power. People are given a positive way of dealing with self-identity.

They also have a way of dealing with the self in relation to others. To live the spiritual life is to be related to God, with this relationship as the basis for all human relationships. To see the image of the Creator in each created being is to have a perspective from which to live among other human beings. The spiritual life, particularly through the forms of prayer, cannot be lived in a possessive sense of closeness to God. The intercessory nature of prayer is a mark of authentic spirituality. Through God, all people are linked to one another in every need, wherever in the world they live, and whatever their condition in life. When *The Book of Common Prayer*, in Elizabethan language, bade a congregation pray for "the whole state of Christ's Church and the world," the reference was to health and wholeness. The petitions begin with the prayer for the universal church, then turn specifically to all ministers, the congregation, and governing authorities. The congregation asks that all people may know and serve God, and prays for those in need, and for those who have died and entered eternal life. One cannot pray this way continually without becoming acutely aware of the universality of interrelationships among people. Learning how to pray in this manner is education for the spiritual life.

Those committed to the spiritual life also learn the relationship of human beings to the rest of the created universe. They develop something of Teilhard de Chardin's awareness that Christ suffuses the universe and that not only the inhabited earth but worlds as yet unknown are the arena of God's redemptive love.[10] No narrow devotion this, but one that places the human being a divine perspective. Far from demeaning men, women, and children, it lifts them into the kind of humanity that in the mystery of God is linked with the divine nature. Human power is seen in a new perspective. The exercise of power is known, in its truest sense, to be a gift of God and a responsibility from God.

The quest for the spiritual life leads one into an understanding of God that cannot be obtained in any other way. Martin Buber's now classic study *I and Thou*[11] brought a concern for relationships into popular religious focus (although it is a book so concisely written that one would hardly call it easy to read). There is a cognitive way of knowing about someone that provides important knowledge, obtainable from books, from a person's work, and from people who have known the person. This is knowledge at second hand from the actual person and provides an I-it relationship. One may also become distanced from a person by observing the person objectively but never entering into any relationship. The I-Thou relationship, by contrast, is the knowledge obtained when a person reveals herself or himself directly to another person. Such knowledge is never complete, because no person is ever completely self-revealing.

God is self-revealed in the Bible, through words and activity. For Christians, God is further self-revealed through Jesus Christ. God is self-revealed through the relationship nurtured in the spiritual quest. God instructs; the believer learns. This is one important way by which human questions about God are answered: questions about God's love, justice, mercy, knowledge, and power.

Education for the spiritual life can effectively help people establish patterns of living that will increase self-awareness and sensitivity to the needs of others. People learn how to deal with anxiety and hostility from the perspective of an ongoing relationship to God that enables them to find the uses for anxiety and the causes of hostility. They learn to link the human desire for power with the dynamic activity of the Holy Spirit— power employed in the service of God. This way does not come naturally, for we are taught that our first parents by their disobedience sought the power that would come with the knowledge to discern good and evil. Only when power is recognized as a gift of God can it co-exist with a serenity that is one mark of the spiritual life.

Living in the presence of God helps people develop attitudes that are attuned more closely to the purposes of God for the world: living for the fulfillment of the Rule of God proclaimed in scripture.

Teresa of Avila, a great guide in the spiritual path, affirmed that Christ has no hands but ours to do his work. Francis of Assisi prayed, "Make me an instrument of your peace," and continued by describing what that would mean in terms of sowing gentleness, reconciliation, and love. These two are called "mystics," a term that some people interpret to mean an otherworldly existence apart from ordinary life. In fact, Teresa was one of the most active of persons, spending a lifetime reforming Carmelite convents in Spain during the sixteenth century. Her spirituality was expressed in her deeds. Francis carried the implications of his prayer to the point where he, a Christian during the period of the Crusades, dared to visit the court of Saladin, the Moslem ruler against whom the Christian princes of Europe were arrayed, to bring a message of peace and reconciliation.

Those who dare open themselves to education for spiritual growth will find themselves propelled toward deeds that may sometimes go against the grain of earlier training or present social realities. This is one of the risks incurred.

Places of Training

The process of education for the spiritual life is not new. It may seem new to people who do not know its history, or are unfamiliar with any religious tradition in which it has been a motivating force. It invites learners to take part in training as arduous as that of the athlete for the faith described by the apostle Paul in 1 Corinthians 9:24–27.

The primary focus of education in the spiritual life has traditionally been the monastery. Buddhism and Christianity both have a long history of monasticism. Many aspects of the training of a monastic, from entrance (the novitiate) through the probationary period, until acceptance and the profession of vows, is similar in both traditions. In recent years, monastics from Roman Catholic and Buddhist traditions have been meeting to share insights. The late Thomas Merton died while attending such a conference at Bangkok in 1968.

Christian monasticism began in the East, with men who aspired toward holiness leaving the cities to live in the desert in Egypt and later in other areas of the Middle East. Some preferred to live alone; others lived in groups. They were supported by townspeople who brought them food. Their life was centered primarily in prayer, usually performed alone, and sometimes with the rest of the community. Western monasticism, beginning with the group gathered around Benedict in the sixth century, was essentially community oriented. Each person had a cell for the hours of sleep and meditation, and all gathered together for meals and worship. The three bases of Benedict's rule were work, study, and prayer. Women's orders were developed with a similar rule.

Several aspects of this education in spirituality should be noted. The community gathered for worship once during each four-hour period, both day and night. Five of these services consisted of chanting from the Psalms, hearing scripture, and praying. Once each day the Eucharist was celebrated. This constant meditation on scripture—especially the Psalms—as an avenue for devotion, was an ever-deepening source of spirituality. The daily Eucharist lifted them into an awareness of the transcendent glory of the risen Lord. Meals were eaten in silence, accompanied by the reading aloud of devotional literature by a person designated to do so. Usually such reading was not heavy theological material, but texts that could be heard easily, such as the lives of the saints, who were held up as models for living. Finally, there were the hours of prayer alone, during which each monk or nun cultivated a personal relationship to God. Fed by regular recourse to the Psalms and other scriptures used in the daily offices and by sharing in the Eucharist, these people were using spiritual resources to deepen prayer, as prayer in turn deepened their understanding of worship. Such was the daily life of the professed monk or nun.

In order to be able to live this kind of life, so different from the ordinary lives of men and women "in the world," each aspirant went through a period of probation under the guidance of a novice master or mistress who taught the monastic way, helped develop the understanding of worship, and enabled each by close and careful guidance to become proficient in the life of prayer. The methods of monastic training have been changed across the centuries, but the basic outline of preparation for what has technically been called "religious life" (as contrasted with "secular life") has remained stable. This has always been recognized as a special way of life, not suitable for everyone. Other Christians living more fully "in the world" have been strengthened by the awareness that in the monastic enclave were some persons deliberately set apart, constantly interceding before God for the needs of the whole world, linking everyone around the world in prayer, and exemplifying the biblical dictum to "pray without ceasing." Moreover, their lives of service, whether to the immediate community, or in works of mercy wherever communities of a religious order were established, have been a powerful form of Christian witness.

Education for spirituality has also been carried on in the

theological seminaries, where clergy have been prepared to exercise their calling. The kind of education has varied with the particular Christian tradition. For some there might be an emphasis on personal Bible reading and prayer, on scripture services and daily preaching, and on forms of mutual witness and sharing. That is essentially an evangelical way. For others, particularly in the Roman Catholic, Orthodox, and Anglican traditions, the emphasis has been more particularly on the daily Eucharistic liturgy and the scripture offices. Roman Catholic seminaries have continued, but modified in number, the offices for worship used in the monastery. Anglicans traditionally used the offices of morning and evening prayer, although these are less used today. The spiritual director has been an important person in the training of priests, guiding seminarians in the development of the devotional life. In recent years the methods of spiritual direction have changed in keeping with the needs of people in this time, but the goals remain the same.[12] We shall be saying more about spiritual direction later in this book.

Education for the spiritual life is also an integral part of certain Protestant religious communities. Such communities are the Protestant equivalents of the monastic communities, and while they have been in existence since the seventeenth century, none that exist today has had a continuous existence from that time. The Community of Brethren, for example, represents a pietistic Anabaptist tradition. Founded in Germany early in the twentieth century, members moved to England during World War II, later settled briefly in South America, and today have several communities in the United States. These are communities of families, each of whom has small family living quarters, although they eat some meals in common. Work is assigned for everyone. There is a common treasury, and education is provided within the community for children through eighth grade, after which they go outside to schools. The basis for the spiritual life is an agreed-upon pattern of living exemplifying the gospel teaching. Members meet for common celebrations, Sunday worship, and special gatherings for shared confession and reconciliation. Baptism and the Lord's Supper are also communal acts of worship. Members educate each other in the spiritual life through personal witness and sharing within the group, and train their children in the community's life and worship.

This survey indicates that education for the spiritual life has a long history among specialized groups. Not until recently has there been so much interest in books and other ways to help people learn about the many aspects of spirituality in various settings. As individuals. members of family groups, and members of churches, many today sense a need to find ways for education in the spiritual life suitable to our situation at the end of the twentieth century.

2. The Process of Spiritual Growth

Many people have reported some dramatic experience of transcendence that gave a different quality to life than they had ever previously known. Others know only the quiet continuity of living. But for both, spiritual growth has continued to be a process. A process implies formation, shaping, and development, however open-ended the goal. People engaged in this process will have some idea of the kinds of persons they hope to become, the way they expect to act in relation to other people, or the steps in the deepening of their relationship to God. They cannot comprehend the complete results because they are aware that human beings do not know fully the intentions of God. They do know some of the ways by which the process of spiritual growth develops.

Spiritual Growth Through Example

One of the basic ways of achieving spiritual growth is through the example of spiritually aware persons. This is a kind of "osmosis" through which a person interiorizes the lifestyle of another person or group by being in the company of that person or that community. Both in Christianity and Buddhism, the monastery has been this kind of community. People desiring to commit themselves to a life of spirituality have found in the monastery an environment in which this became possible, nourished by careful formation, a way of life that left time for the cultivation of the spiritual life, and the example of those who practiced it. In Eastern Christianity, however, although there are monastic communities, there is also the Russian Orthodox *staretz*, a holy man or woman who lives an itinerant existence among the villages, attracting those who either seek inspiration for daily living from the example and counsel of such a person, or who become a companion and follower with the intention of becoming, in turn, a *staretz*.

The now-classic devotional book *The Way of a Pilgrim* chronicles the life of such a person.[1] Following a brief marriage and the early death of his wife, the Pilgrim vowed to live a life of utter simplicity, focusing every moment on God and depending for the necessities of life on the goodwill of the villagers as he journeyed from place to place. Drawn by his simple goodness, his imperviousness to cold, hunger, or any other hardship, people came to him for advice, consolation, and encouragement. The basis for his own devotional life was a simple sentence, known as the Jesus Prayer. It is a variant of the *Kyrie eleison*, the cry of praise and prayer that has been part of the liturgy since at least the fourth century. The pilgrim prayed, "Lord Jesus Christ, son of the living God, have mercy on me, a sinner." Ceaselessly, he repeated these words, a type of Christian mantra. The rhythm of the repetition lifted him beyond self. Meditation on individual words and phrases emphasized the many meanings of the prayer. The Pilgrim began his spiritual journey by following a *staretz*, and he in turn became one. Thus the chain of spirituality was nurtured and passed on from one generation to the next, and the spirituality of the people of the villages was enhanced beyond that which came to them from the more ordinary experiences of parish life.

Monastics in the Western Christian tradition functioned similarly for the people whose lives they touched. They too were sometimes hermits, living alone, but related to a particular village church or monastery somewhat more than was the *staretz*. Such a hermit was Julian of Norwich. Suffused with the adoration that she experienced through the maternal love of Jesus, she was an inspiration to the villagers, and in particular to Margery Kempe, to whom she became an exemplar. Julian has given reassurance to countless people through the often-quoted sentence from her visions, "And all shall be well, and all shall be well, and all manner of things shall be well."[2]

People in the Western tradition have long known about Francis of Assisi, who turned from a life of luxury to one of voluntary poverty with the intention of sharing his possessions with the poor. He became an example to the townspeople of the biblical assurance that God provides. Francis attracted others to his way of life and soon the order of mendicant friars was begun.[3] A sister order was established by Clare, to whom Francis was friend and mentor. In the hymn of praise attributed to Francis, God is exalted for all the elements of the created world, of which Francis views humans as one part. He places human life in the perspective of God's whole creation and asserts a relationship of kinship among all the elements. The example of his life in the embrace of Lady Poverty, as he said, drew others to him, and the Franciscan order increased in numbers. His was the first of the monastic groups to develop a spiritual life that was lived as much in the world as it was withdrawn into the quiet life.

The pietistic Protestant tradition produced Count Nikolaus Ludwig von Zinzendorf (1700–1760), who drew around him on his estates in Saxony the remnants of the Unitas Fratrum, a group in exile from Bohemia. Under his leadership they became a community of families and from them developed what later became the Moravian Church. With ecumenical dreams beyond his time and the kind of devotion to Jesus that frequently characterized the pietistic tradition, he gathered a people who forged a faith that included theological and liturgical elements from both the Lutheran and Calvinist traditions. This mixture of faiths, in a time of rigid distinctions among religious groups, alientated the Moravians from both communities and they finally found refuge in America. Devoted to peace and to a simple life, they named one of their settlements Bethlehem (Pennsylvania), and another Salem (North Carolina). They have continued to be models for a specific devotional lifestyle.

The Society of Friends, commonly called the Quakers, were another Protestant group that drew people into its own form of spiritual life. The Society began with the preaching of George Fox in England in the seventeenth century (1624–1676)[4] and, like the Franciscans and the Moravians, its members devoted themselves to a life of simplicity and peacefulness. One of the most remarkable of the Friends was Elizabeth Gurney Fry (1780–1845), who exemplified their emphasis on living by the example of Jesus. In addition to raising a large family, this daughter and wife of wealthy London merchants single-handedly initiated and caused the implementation of efforts to reform the prison system in England. These reforms spread to the continent even during her lifetime. Similarly, in the United States, Dorothea Lynde Dix (1802–1887) spearheaded a movement for the establishment of hospitals for the mentally ill, who were at the time being held in prisons. The admonition to see Christ in the neighbor and to serve all who were in need has been basic to the Quaker tradition from its earliest days to the present. For many years the American Friends Service Committee has provided an avenue for this form of witness.

Living in the presence of such a person as Francis of Assisi, Julian of Norwich, Nikolaus von Zinzendorf, or Elizabeth Fry would be an inspiration. Their vision of the Christian life was shared by people who knew them. In addition, each had connections with others who held the same vision of life. For Francis and von Zinzendorf, these others were part of their communities. For Julian it was the people who set themselves apart for the reclusive life, and for Fry it was the congregation with whom she worshipped and whose way of life she sought to exemplify. To be sure, only those who were attracted by their life and work would admire them and want to be like them. Most people simply ignored what they saw, and some actively opposed their work.

To watch such a person at work was to be blessed by the

presence of God, whose Spirit was acting in and through that person. No more powerful way for spiritual development could be found. Even those who did not feel that their family obligations left them free to follow in a literal sense nevertheless knew that God was present, and that they too could develop a lifestyle consonant with that presence.

Some became disciples consciously. They gave up everything to follow, whether by becoming a Franciscan, a Moravian, or a Friend—or by commitment to a similarly consecrated community. In order that such a common life can develop, a guiding rule is needed that describes the intention and ways by which this intention can be lived. Each day will include a time of meditation on the intention, on one's personal strength and weaknesses within that framework, and the spiritual resources available for strengthening.

The spiritual mentor helps learners to understand wisdom. A medium frequently employed is a manual for the devotional life, many of which have been preserved for centuries. Some are still being written. The exemplar or mentor teachers the disciple how to pray, how to deepen the times of meditation, how to conform life practices to the religious life of the community, and how to desire what is professed, so that life is lived in joyous acceptance of a Way rather than in rigid conformity to a Rule.

Spiritually aware persons assist others by a willingness to share the struggles of their own journey and to recount failures as well as successes, difficulties as well as progress. No one person can replicate the experience of another, but it is reassuring to know that the person who seems to have achieved some proficiency may have come to this point through a long process of sensitization to the work of God's Holy Spirit.

It becomes clear, then, that one element in education for the spiritual life is through the example of particular persons whose presence and lifestyle inspire others. To be in their presence, watch them at work, absorb their words of wisdom, hear the recital of their experiences, and deliberately to fashion a life after their example, are ways in which a one person becomes spiritually deepened through another.

Spiritual Growth Through a Tradition

The existence of a conscious tradition of spirituality is an important element in the development of the knowledge and the desire for such spirituality in an individual. Mention has already been made of the encouragement given to those persons perceived as being set apart by their holiness in the Russian Orthodox religious tradition. So it was in an earlier time, when caves near the River Nile in Egypt sheltered holy men, and other places in the Middle Eastern deserts became home to similar hermits. The model for Eastern monasticism was the rule of St. Basil the Great (330–379).

The earliest formal monastic community in Western Christendom is credited to the work of Benedict of Nursia (480–547), although there were small communities earlier, such as the group of monks gathered around Jerome in Bethlehem, with a similar community of nuns nearby. As new communities formed in the late Middle Ages, each was established to cultivate a specific form of spirituality. The work of the Augustinians was to preach the gospel and evangelize. The Cistercians lived in silence, gathering only for praise and prayer at the Eucharistic liturgy and the daily offices. The Carthusians rarely gather, deeming the work of solitary intercessory prayer to be their appropriate expression of the Christian life. The Carmelites, reformed by Teresa of Avila, are a similarly enclosed order for women.

An example of the monastic life is conveyed to children at schools where they are taught by members of a particular religious order. Some orders were founded expressly for teaching, as others were founded to do hospital work, visiting, or assisting the poor. Through contacts with members of religious orders, young people are motivated to explore for themselves the possibilities and some are drawn to such a vocation. Participation in either a highly structured community, or one where members carry on their work in missions throughout society, has brought inner freedom, fulfillment, and opportunities for service through dedication to a rule and acceptance of life vows. Until the twentieth century the opportunities available for women have been more varied for members of religious orders than for women accepting the traditional patterns of marriage and family. This is evident in a comparison of the roles of Protestant and Catholic women in European and American society from the sixteenth century to the twentieth century. The religious community provided for its members seclusion for cultivating the devotional life, and specific avenues of service to express their devotion.

Most of the world's religions have developed forms of communal living. Gautama the Buddha gathered monks and gave them the rules by which they lived. (This contrasts with the less formal relationship between Jesus and his disciples.) Basically the life of the Buddhist monk is one of renunciation and detachment from the world so that neither pain or pleasure can affect one's serenity. Hindu monasticism, which developed later, has been less structured. Like the Buddhist monk, the Hindu goes among the people daily to beg for food, and the people feel blessed by this opportunity for service. The work of the monks is in their lives of devotion and the study of scripture.

Within Judaism, with its strong emphasis on family life, only the Essenes were a celibate and ascetical community, set apart for the spiritual life. Possibly the Qumran community, to whom the Dead Sea Scrolls belonged, were from this background.

Some communities maintain a rule of life but are also active in society. Sufism is a mystical order within Islam that emphasizes the spiritual immediacy of the presence of God, in contrast to the formal scriptural orthodoxy of Islam. Noted for its ecstatic dance of praise, the group was established by Mevlana Jalludin at Konya in the thirteenth century.

The Protestant pietistic traditions have seen the development of other religious movements in addition to that of the

Moravians. John Wesley's spiritual struggles eventuated in the beginnings of the Methodist movement, whose class meetings of small groups of converted people met for mutual witness, to encourage one another in their assurance of salvation, and to cultivate the spiritual life. The Methodists did not live in isolated communities. They gathered from their ordinary work and family lives to form these groups for mutual strengthening. Their piety, along with John Wesley's preaching and Charles Wesley's hymnody, brought a new spirit that swept like wildfire throughout England, reviving religious life.

Methodism crossed the Atlantic to awaken the spiritual life of America through the itinerant ministry of George Whitefield. The Wesleyan spirituality that became a renewing environment for believers brought the joyous experience of having obtained salvation through Jesus Christ, and the continuing realization of the immediacy of the Holy Spirit, with the possibility of Christian perfection through the continuing work of the Spirit. The class meeting was a medium through which people assisted one another in the spiritual quest. Later, after the break with the Church of England, the form of the worship service, particularly in America, came to represent the spiritual life of the community through the emphasis on hymns, prayer, preaching, and witness. The revival meeting, especially in the form of the camp meeting that met in one location for a number of days, was another form of spiritual renewal.

Some Anabaptist church groups and, more specifically, the Amish, exhibit still another form of culture through which spiritual growth develops. Although they live in towns where not everyone is Amish, they have usually moved there as a company of families. Their life of simplicity witnesses to their understanding of biblical teaching. They reject nineteenth- and twentieth-century inventions, living without electricity or automobiles. They cultivate the land with a faithful sense of being stewards of God's created earth. They educate their children for that particular way of life, so seeing no need for education beyond the elementary level. They gather for worship in a meetinghouse as simple as their homes. For them, as for other religious groups, the form and content of worship both exemplify and reinforce their beliefs and the way they live. When a family is in need, everyone helps: building a barn, rebuilding a house after a fire, or gathering the crops when a farmer becomes disabled. Mutual service is as much a part of their life as it is of monks or nuns living in community.

Such examples indicate that the tradition of a shared spiritual culture is a powerful tool for spiritual development. The people who hold a tradition in common are examples to one another. They also encourage one another, because it is easier to maintain a given way of life in the company of others than it is to do so alone. They consciously educate people, particularly their own children (or novices in an order), to accept their pattern of living. They develop guiding rules that provide both flexibility and boundaries. They provide forms of worship that express their understanding of who God is and how God acts. They develop personal devotional practices that train people in particular interpretations of the relationship to God. This is a total education for the spiritual life.

Spiritual Growth Through Formation

The spiritual person and the spiritual community are both agents of formation, but they accomplish this formation most completely when there is a conscious effort to assist individuals in the development of the spiritual life. This development is accomplished through a careful "mix" of learning about the spiritual life and living it. Anyone can become immersed in books about prayer. These may engender an objective attitude by which the reader learns about a process called prayer, but there would be no need to engage in the practice of prayer. In fact, the practice of prayer is generated not so much by a knowledge of techniques as through a relationship to the living God.

The nature of this relationship, as understood by a particular religious congregation, is obvious to a visitor at a church service or in a Sunday school class. For some the forms of prayer are uniformly introspective and personal without any seeming awareness of the spiritual power of transformation through intercessory prayer in behalf of people and events both near and far. For others they are far-ranging. Some emphasize thanksgiving, others petition. Neither theory nor practice alone will do more than provide an individual with limited insight. Reading about prayer is a link with people who have developed their spiritual life. Many lived centuries ago. Some are living and writing today. The reader does not know them personally, but becomes acquainted with them through a common quest. Practice of the spiritual life can flow from reading about it, as one becomes attuned to the insights of the writer, and begins to use these for one's own spiritual development.

Several writings designed to assist individuals in this spiritual growth have come to us from the eighteenth century. Francis de Sales, spiritual director to a woman of the French nobility, wrote *Introduction to the Devout Life*.[5] Consider Mme. Jeanne de Chantal, caught up in a busy social life, close to the court and its politics and responsible for the governance of a household, yet seeking to live a religious life outside the environment of a convent. De Sales addressed his counsel to women in this kind of situation. One can hear in the letters her questions and his replies. This kind of writing is eminently practical because of its direct address. The continuing popularity of this particular writing suggest that Mme. de Chantal's experience had much in common with that of other people endeavoring to cultivate the spiritual life while enveloped in the busyness of secular concerns.

A similar writing is that of Archbishop François Fenelon to Jeanne-Marie Guyon, a devout noblewoman in seventeenth-century France. Mme. Guyon sought a spiritual path to perfection. She hoped through contemplation to be enabled to yield herself so completely to the will of God that her own will, totally absorbed by the divine purpose, should no longer exist.

This intense form of spirituality, known as Quietism, was condemned by the church, which affirmed the active participation of the believer in the development of spirituality. Fenelon's writing concerning the adoration and pure love of God have, however, been helpful to readers for three centuries. As spiritual director to another noblewoman, the Countess of Gramonte, he wrote on "The Need of Devotion in a Worldly Life":

> October 2, 1689.
> It seems to me, Madame, that you have two things to do—one with respect to your engagements, the other with respect to yourself. The first consists in the care you should take to redeem some brief time from the world for reading and prayer. Try to rescue half an hour morning and evening. You must learn, too, to make good use of chance moments—when waiting for someone, when going from place to place, or when in society, where to be a good listener is all that is required. One raises one's heart for an instant to God and renews one's strength for further duties.[6]

In the twentieth-century Quaker tradition, a small book by Thomas Kelly entitled *A Testament of Devotion* has deepened the spiritual life of numerous people.[7] By sharing the depths and heights as well as the plateaus of his own journeying, Kelly has given assurance to readers on their spiritual journey. Growth in spirituality today follows much the same process as it did for those seventeenth-century women for whom their spiritual directors wrote: that of reading, praying, reflecting, and living. There is continuous interaction between learning about and doing in the spiritual life.

Formation also includes a conscious effort to develop. This statement goes counter to a viewpoint that holds the spiritual life to be spontaneous. In a sense it is spontaneous, in that the spiritual life is life lived entirely in the presence of God, and there is a necessary spontaneity in all good relationships. Beyond that, however, is the cultivation and expansion of a relationship. This cultivation makes the difference between a totally interior spirituality like that of Mme. Guyon, who wanted only to lose her will in the will of God, and an outgoing spirituality that finds its expression in Francis of Assisi, daring to go into enemy territory for love of God and to beg for peace among all God's children. Living is in constant interaction with and reflection upon learning, whether that learning comes through the example of a person, life in a community, or reading devotional literature—including the scriptures. These elements help people put together a routine for spiritual living.

If the word "routine" sounds too stereotyped, too monotonous, call this a pattern, or even the flow of the day. Every life has such a pattern, but most people simply take this for granted. If they were to analyze a day's activities, they would know immediately the relations among work, play, personal reflection, and relationships with others. The person desiring to develop the spiritual life looks at this pattern to examine in what ways it nurtures spiritual growth and in what ways in inhibits growth.

Perhaps analyzing a day at a time may be too rigid. For some the pattern of life may be a weekly one. Whatever the direction, it is necessary to discover time for specific spiritual nurturing, and to engage in activities through which the spiritual dimension of life can transform the actions themselves.

Manuals on prayer analyze both the nature of this activity and methods for its development. Without the rigidity of time limits, each person needs to become aware of the necessity for time alone to hear and respond to God. The place of silent meditation and spoken prayer is related to the time made available. Some people find the frustrations of waiting, whether at home or at work, to be transformed by using these moments for quiet recall of the presence of God. Others find that some of the day's activities are routine, and do not demand concentrated attention. Such times can be used for recalling scripture, or engaging in meditation and prayer.

The pattern for living should also include time for reading and serious study through which the Bible and other religious writings can help form the spiritual life. Reading the Bible and receiving it as God's word has traditionally preceded prayer, which is the response to God. Early risers may read the Bible before the day's work begins. Others will read and meditate on scripture before sleep. Any of the hours between may become the "best" time for some people. The experience and advice to be found in spiritual writings can be a helpful enrichment for personal practice. For those who are becoming advanced in spiritual training, the daily newspaper may become a means for hearing the word of God. Daily work, as has been pointed out, may include elements of the divine or the demonic. Work may become transformed by an awareness of the transcendent possibilities. Or demonic elements may become so evident that a decision will need to be made as to whether such work can enhance the spiritual quality of lives, or become destructive of human beings. The ancient monastic tradition of work, study, and prayer has a counterpart in the ordinary lives of women, men, and children. Time for oneself, a pause to stretch the body by exercise of some kind, may become a time for deepened awareness of the wonder of the body as God's creation, and joy in this gift through which life is embodied.

Finally, if the routine of living is to deepen spiritual growth, this will include participation in a worshipping congregation. Spirituality is never complete when it involves only a personal relationship to God. No human being ever possessed God, but an accent on personal devotion alone could foster that illusion. The church's worship to praise and prayer is an essential element in spiritual development. The individual is strengthened by the presence of other believers. One is taught scripture by listening to readings from the Bible; one learns how to pray by participating in the prayer of the people of God. Through worship one learns the meaning of giving and is strengthened by participation in the Lord's Supper, whatever the form taken by a particular liturgy.

Spiritual growth develops through years devoted to nurturing a lifestyle of quiet, gentleness, and sensitivity to God and other people. Spiritually mature persons are dynamically active and aggressively involved in life, but they also exhibit a particular kind of quietness that indicates strength. The psalmist writes, "In quietness and in confidence shall be your strength." Through quietness of mind, one is enabled to "hear" other people, and to "hear" and respond to the leading of God. Men and women in religious orders have been examples of this approach. So have the Quakers, with their active pacifism and their willingness to be persecuted for what they believe to be righteousness' sake.

Spiritual Growth and the Work of the Holy Spirit

The foregoing examples could leave the impression that spiritual growth is completely a human endeavor. Yet the very words "spirit" and "spiritual" suggest the work of God's Holy Spirit. In all religious traditions, spirituality is the work of divine transformation. This puts the human effort in perspective.

Spiritual growth begins with an openness to God, which places God at the center of life but at the same time recognizes that God transcends human limitations. This openness requires the relaxation of barriers and a letting go of personal intentions. A flexibility is developed that makes possible the facing of any eventuality, knowing that God works through events rather than counter to events. Being open to God limits the determination to plan one's life totally, yet permits a sense of life direction. In being open to God and aware of the presence of God, a person is prevented from developing the idea that techniques alone are the key to a fully spiritual growth—and that God could be manipulated by human means.

Openness includes a questing spirit. The picture of the quest is that of a journey. One is certain where it will end, but never knows what experiences will be found along the path. Don Quixote goes on such a journey. His creator, Miguel de Cervantes, was writing a not-so-gentle satire of how he viewed people. John Bunyan's Christian is on a journey in *Pilgrim's Progress.* Through temptations and unhappy experiences

Christian stands steadfast in the faith until crossing through the dark waters of Jordan into the celestial city. The people of Israel were on journey from Egypt into their promised land. Their faith was sometimes tried and found wanting, but their leader, Moses, was steadfast, as was the appointed successor, Joshua.

Christians view life as following in the steps of Jesus. For them comes the angelic song of glory and a joyful revelation of God. They too are baptized and tempted. For them the years of life are times of discipleship, while learning what it means to call Jesus Lord. Most profoundly, the Christian journey is to follow along the way of the Cross. This way gives meaning to suffering, strange as it may seem to nonbelievers. The mystery of unjust suffering is found in the humiliation, degradation, and sense of abandonment, even by God. Through such identification with Jesus the Christian accepts the Calvary of failure and death, because the Resurrection lies on the other side of crucifixion.

When spiritual development is perceived in the form of quest, one expects to be surprised. Life will not go according to plan, but somehow it will be liveable. Surprise may be joyous, lifting a person to the heights of happiness. Surprise may plunge a person into the depths of despair. There is no certainty as to how an event will end. What can be expected is the continuing sense of God's presence as the foundation for life. Advent, as was pointed out earlier, is a season of expectation. But that which is awaited eagerly may, in biblical terms, bring either a judgment of bliss ("enter into the joy of the Lord") or of retribution ("be cast into outer darkness"). The spiritual person need not fear the judgment. Tried in the fiery furnace, the gold is refined.

People on a quest must be willing to live with uncertainty. This runs counter to all the human need for security discussed in Chapter 1. Uncertainty arises from the frustrated desire to formulate plans, work toward goals, and find satisfaction in their fulfillment. God may seem to thwart well-intentioned plans and completely change the goals. No wonder there is an urge to give up. This does not suggest the serenity toward which the spiritual life is supposed to lead. The ability to accept uncertainty tests one's openness to God, which is a mark of the spiritual life. The believer knows that there is no uncertainty with God, however God may interact with the sometimes obstructing actions of human beings.

Spiritual growth is a combination of "nature" and "nurture." God has endowed people with many kinds of gifts. Paul writes of the gifts given for the upbuilding of the church. There may also be varieties in the gifts of spirituality available to people. There may be differences in the degree of spiritual formation possible to each person. An acceptance of this possibility would prevent people from striving fruitlessly to achieve some ideal goal. They could, instead, be content with the apprehension of God available at any given time. The acceptance of a personal measure of spiritual development would break away from the competitive striving that is a hallmark of Western society. Because no one knows the fullness of an individual's potential, there is no need to settle at any one level. Nor is there need to strive beyond the assurance of the divine relationship revealed at any point in time, and the life that is being lived under the impetus of that relationship.

However attuned to the spiritual a person may be, growth in the Spirit includes nurture. God works quietly, imperceptibly, on a level frequently unrecognized. There are many avenues through which this growth can take place. They do not depend for efficacy on some perceived level of spiritual awareness but on the individual's continuing involvement in spiritual growth. The life with God is cultivated, as is any other relationship. God is the initiator, but the human response is essential. That response may be natural in the sense that one believes humans to be born with capacities for spiritual growth, but it develops as part of a fully maturing life. Charles M. Magsam, writing about contemporary spirituality, states:

Maturity is a continuous development: it is not something we come to at some magical moment and stay in for the rest of our lives. There is a maturity proper and possible at every stage of life. . . . We are mature when we are still teachable, quick to learn, flexible.[8]

This interaction of nature and nurture makes spiritual maturity possible.

Spiritual growth includes an awareness of the ambiguities in the working of the Holy Spirit. We do not own God, and cannot foresee how God's Spirit will be revealed. Some actions to which a person is impelled may seem strange to other people. Francis of Assisi puzzled the people who knew him. Teresa of Avila angered her nuns by the reforms she ordered. The visions of Mother Ann that formed the foundation for Shaker communities seemed strange to American villagers. It is one mark of the spiritual quest that insights may seem more puzzling than enlightening. Trusted friends may believe that the inspiration has been mistaken. When Jesus, on the road to Jerusalem, confided to the disciples that his life was drawing to a close, faithful Peter, of all people, assured him that this could not be so, and drew upon himself the rebuke that he, the disciple, was a voice for Satan. How then does one know from whom the voice comes? This is the ambiguity of the Spirit. One must live with that and believe.

The work of the Holy Spirit in spiritual growth is basic to any understanding of the religious life. One whole dimension of such growth may be seen in the pentecostal movement from the first generation of the church to the present time. The tongues of flame, the speaking in tongues, the many visible and sometimes astounding if not violent workings of the Spirit are a whole subject in themselves. The apostle Paul warns a congregation to test the spirits, and the church has been doing so ever since that time. Sometimes the testing process has pitted congregations against individuals, or placed judicatories in opposition to congregations. This is a troublesome matter. In truth, the Spirit of God cannot be contained nor domesticated. What then are the limitations by which a person or church knows whose work is being proclaimed? The answer is not easy.

Aspects of Education in the Spirit

To summarize what is being said in this chapter, several aspects of the process of spiritual growth need recapitulation. It is important to live in a culture that encourages and expects growth in the spiritual life. Some formulations of Christianity have laid greater emphasis on belief structures that bind the group together than on the more individualized aspects of spiritual formation. The possibility of divergent insights coming through "inspiration" have made leaders wary of individualized expressions of faith. Such a concern motivated the Inquisition in sixteenth-century Spain, with the imprisonment of John of the Cross and the warnings to Teresa of Avila, who found it expedient not to publish her works. Calvinist Boston a century later acted on parallel grounds in its persecution of Quakers and the eventual execution of Mary Dyer.

Other formulations of Christianity may stress a particular way of life and may hold the spiritual quest to be an avoidance of the hard realities of Christian action, such as the traditional Wesleyan Methodists, who emphasize a particular mode of living. The Arminian understanding of the responsibility of the believer in the process of salvation (free will) can lead to an underestimate of freedom in the Spirit. From a different theological perspective, the liberal wing of Protestant Christianity has emphasized principles of social justice that may appear to subordinate people to ideals and to disparage the seeming unreality of the spiritual and the mystical. This is ironic in that the emphasis on social gospel derives from philosophical idealism, which itself has an element of the abstractly perfect.

If one views the spiritual life as veering toward the mystical experience of God, which it may legitimately do, then Judaism has not usually encouraged this expression of spirituality. The Hasidic movement, beginning with Rabbi Bal Shem in the seventeenth century has found a powerful proponent in Martin Buber's concept of I and Thou.[9] Islam has a concreteness that does not encourage the mystical either. The Sufis are the mystically oriented group within Islam.

Some form of spiritual life is practiced by all religious groups. The forms considered here seem to flourish most fully in a culture that encourages silence as a pathway to God. In Christian traditions, this has been cultivated within the Orthodox and Roman Catholic traditions, where members of monastic orders are respected for their unique way of life. Among Protestants, forms of spiritual practice developed in particular groups, which in their own way correspond to religious orders, such as the Society of Friends, the Amish, and others. Any Christian tradition could encourage this approach, and there seems to be some interest today in reclaiming this heritage. An expectation of particular forms of spiritual development will result in concrete ways of encouraging such development.

In the 1960s, religious as well as secular communities of young people encouraged a self-sufficient lifestyle that turned away from society as they knew it in order to develop an inwardness centered in the group. This approach is less evident today. Religious and secular communities have continued to develop within established traditions, although in freer patterns than were permitted in the past, as may be observed in changes in the work, dress, and living patterns within Roman Catholic orders.

Living in a group that values the cultivation of the spiritual life means that persons are approved of and encouraged in their development. Such a culture provides models and mentors of the spiritual life. An important element in any education is the persons through whom the young are taught. The Christian tradition is filled with such people. Their story is important in the education of those in each generation. The daily life of living Christians is also important. Seldom do we become aware of such people in their own times. Today we recount the lives of Dorothy Day, Simone Weil, Martin Luther King, Jr.,

Thomas Merton, and in the Jewish tradition, Martin Buber.

Each congregation includes such people. Frequently, theirs are hidden lives, for who is so confident as to admit to proficiency in the spiritual life? Yet such people are the exemplars and teachers. They are important as guides and need to know themselves called to this educational work. They can make available to others the spiritual writings that have formed them. They can offer to teach others some of the ways by which their own spiritual life has been deepened. They can share the difficulties of the Way. It would not be easy, but it is a call.

Another aspect of education in the spiritual life is the necessity for learning *about* spirituality. Those whose whole life has been a discipline of devotion have frequently shared their journey and their insights in writing. The classics of spirituality are many. Some are still helpful to people. Spiritual autobiographies encourage us to know that we are not alone: others have been on the quest. Books of meditations lift the reader into the presence of God. Reflections on scripture help others understand how they too can search this treasure for a deeper awareness of life with God. Manuals give specific help in ways of meditation. The *Exercises* of Ignatius Loyola[10] have been rediscovered recently by people who have found his use of imagery helpful. They can put themselves in the picture formed by the recital of a biblical event. Quaker ways of entering into silence as described by Rufus Jones and Elton Trueblood have helped many people develop this side of their spiritual natures. It is important to appropriate the experience of people who can become spiritual guides.

Reading *about* the spiritual life is not enough. Eventually, it must be practiced. There has to be a letting go in which one tries out what others have experienced and appropriates it for one's own life. Relationships are built slowly. Competencies are developed. The spiritual life may begin with one experience of glory, as it did with John Wesley, but it does not end there for the person committed to God. Experiences of high vision are succeeded by walks through the desert, or a seemingly endless journey on the plateau. This is what pilgrimage is all about. The Vision sustains. The Spirit teaches.

The development of piety lies in an openness to the work of the Holy Spirit. The cultivation of God's presence is renewed every day. The Spirit is like the wind, blowing everywhere, alternately still and gusty. The gentle breeze comforts; the gale cannot be contained. So humans, daring to call upon the Spirit, must be ready to accept whatever manifestations are given. It is important to recognize that this aspect of God is unswayed by the desires of human creatures. One is formed through a process of spiritual growth that includes communities, individuals, scripture and other writings, and the action of God, who is both transcendent and immanent.

3. Tracing the Spiritual Way

The yearning for a deeper spiritual life is not new. It is expressed in the sacred writings of all religions. The foundation for Jewish and Christian spirituality is laid in the Bible.

The word "spirituality" seldom appears in the Bible, but the word "spirit" fills many columns in a concordance. The Bible begins with the affirmation that "the Spirit of God was moving over the face of the waters" (Gen. 1:2). By this action of the Spirit chaos was overcome and the world created. What a powerful introduction for all human meditation on life in the Spirit!

The word "spirit" in Hebrew carries the meaning of "breath," with the implication that breath is the essence of life. To breathe is to be alive. Life is the gift of God: the divine life shared with all creation. This first chapter of the Bible ends with human beings created in the image of God (Gen. 2:27).

Statements about the divine spirit and the human spirit are juxtaposed in a passage from the story of Joseph. Pharaoh had a dream and when he awoke "his spirit was troubled" (Gen. 41:8). The dream was interpreted by Joseph to mean that Egypt was entering an era of prosperity (seven good years) to be followed by an era of famine (seven lean years) that would require the service of an astute and honest administrator to keep reserves from the good years in order to ensure survival during the lean years. Pharaoh then asked, "Can we find such a man as this, in whom is the Spirit of God?" (Gen. 41:38). He answered by turning to Joseph as one who would be qualified because God had already shown him how to interpret a dream. The Spirit of God rested upon the interpreter, who had been granted knowledge of God's purposes (Daniel later interpreted the dreams of Nebuchadnezzar, through the power of the Spirit).

All human abilities are divine gifts. We speak of people as being creative, or of having creativity. Theologically speaking, God alone is the Creator, as the originator of the world and all of life. But the Bible affirms a perception of the special quality of human abilities. Just as the Spirit of God was active at the beginning of creation, so it is written later that when the people of Israel encamped near Sinai and were ready to build the tabernacle, God said to Moses that people would be found to do the work. "I have called by name Bezalel . . . and I have filled him with the Spirit of God, with ability and intelligence, with knowledge and all craftsmanship" (Exod. 31:2,3). All people have gifts, but only some rightly recognize these as given by God. This perception makes it possible for individuals to develop their gifts in the conscious recognition of being empowered by the divine Spirit. It is said of the composer Johann Sebastian Bach that he wrote on each manuscript "ad gloriam dei," meaning "to the glory of God." For almost three centuries, people have found their own spiritual lives deepened through Bach's interpretation of the biblical story.

Another evidence of the Spirit of God was the ability to prophesy. This also appears early in the biblical narrative. When Moses, at God's behest, appointed seventy elders to help in the administration of the camp, it is written that the Lord's spirit was upon them, "and when the spirit rested upon them, they prophesied." When two other men also prophesied in the Spirit, Joshua suggested that they be forbidden, but Moses replied, "Would that all the Lord's people were prophets, that the Lord would put his Spirit upon them!" (Num. 11:29). From this time on, the Bible continues to record the existence of Spirit-filled people through whom the word and will of God were made known. Ezekiel's visions were the work of the Spirit. "The Spirit entered me and set me upon my feet" (Ezek. 2:2); "the Spirit took me up" (3:2). After the death of Moses, Joshua, filled with the spirit of wisdom, became their leader. This power had earlier been given him by Moses through the laying on of hands (Deut. 34:9). The charismatic leaders in the book of Judges were Spirit-filled: Othniel, who went to war to release his people from the yoke of Mesopotamia; Gideon, who led them against the Midianites; Jephthah, who fought the Ammonites (and made the tragic vow that doomed his innocent daughter); and Samson, of whom it is several times written that the Spirit of the Lord came upon him, making possible his exploits.

What can be said today about such prompting of the Spirit, and what does this have to do with spirituality? To a casual reader of the Bible, the Spirit of God works *for* a chosen people and *against* people who might interfere with their life; works through people who may have questionable goals and pursue these in devious ways; works harm toward some of God's children in order to benefit others. This appraisal needs to be considered seriously, because questions continue to arise about some activities that are carried out in the name of God. While an answer may be clear to some people that God's ways are not understandable to human beings (God has other purposes for the Mesopotamians or the Midianites) and that everything God does works toward good ends, others will say that if these are the ways in which the God of the Bible acts, such partiality hardly fits the character of One who is called holy. This seeming discrepancy has been explained by saying that the Bible gives theological meaning to historical events. The biblical writers view this partiality as a way through which the divine promise made to Abraham is fulfilled. They view the outcome of events as a vindication of the active presence of the one living God. The hero stories in the Book of Judges illustrate clearly that God uses sinful persons for divine purposes, and that the people who wrote the Book saw God's activity in all human activity. It may be difficult to limit, by definition or description, the working of the Holy Spirit.

The Spirit of God was upon the kings and their anointing was the sign of their election by God to that task. Of Saul it is written both that the Spirit of God was upon him, and later that the Spirit of the Lord departed from him (1 Sam. 16:14), indicating that Saul had been faithless to his calling. Nor did the Spirit rest only on the kings of Israel and Judah. The book of Ezra opens with the words, "In the first year of Cyrus king of Persia, that the word of the Lord by the mouth of Jeremiah might be accomplished, the Lord stirred up the spirit of Cyrus . . . ." (Ezra 1:1). The result was that he gave permission for rebuilding the temple at Jerusalem. Thus what the Spirit had proclaimed through the prophet Jeremiah as God's purpose was fulfilled by an alien king to whom Jeremiah's people were subject.

Moses' hope that all God's people would prophesy is echoed centuries later in Joel's vision of the Day of the Lord in which "it shall come to pass afterward, that I will pour out my spirit on all flesh; your sons and your daughters shall prophesy, your old men shall dream dreams, and your young men shall see visions. Even upon the menservants and the maidservants in those days, I will pour out my spirit" (Joel 2:28–29). In the often-quoted words from the vision of Zechariah to Zerubbabel, "Not by might, nor by power, but by my Spirit, says the Lord of hosts" (Zech. 4:6).

The spiritual life depends upon an incorporation of the spirit of God into an individual's life—and of the Holy Spirit's dwelling within a community. In the Old Testament narratives, the Spirit of God created the world, gave to individuals their gift of intelligence and creativity, bestowed upon leaders their authority to rule, and made it possible for chosen people to make known the will of God as prophecy. There is a persistent suggestion that the Holy Spirit is available to each person when the sense of calling is recognized.

In the New Testament

The gospels convey similar understandings of the ways of the Spirit, but extend some and omit others. In the New Testament, no one indicates that any ruler is acting by the Spirit of God. Political life seems to be quite separate from the life of

the religious community, Jewish or Christian, and even antithetical to it.

The gospels are unequivocal in stating early that the Spirit of
God was upon Jesus. This is indicated in the narratives of his
baptism. The content of the first chapter of Mark is substan-
tially duplicated in the other gospels. When Jesus came up out
of the water, "immediately he saw the heavens opened and the
Spirit descending upon him like a dove" (Mark 1:10). Immediately the Spirit drove him into the wilderness (Mark 1:12).
Luke records how he stood up to read in the synagogue at
Nazareth, where he had been brought up. The lesson that day
was from Isaiah: "The Spirit of the Lord is upon me, because
he has anointed me to preach good news to the poor. He has
sent me to proclaim release to the captives and recovering of
sight to the blind, to set at liberty those who are oppressed, to
proclaim the acceptable year of the Lord" (Luke 4:1619; Isa.
61:1-2). The prophet's comforting vision of good news to his
suffering people is announced by Jesus to have been fulfilled in
his own person. As kings and prophets in the past had been
anointed and gifted with the Spirit for their calling, so Jesus
knew himself to be called. He would be preaching good news
to the poor, proclaiming release to captives, healing the blind,
freeing the oppressed, and proclaiming "the year of the Lord's
favor" (NEB).

This proclamation is demonstrated in the gospel narratives.
Jesus met people in their different needs. He healed some of
diseases; he cast out demons by the power of the spirit. Moreover, reflecting the affirmation in Genesis that human life is
the expression of God's Spirit, the gospels speak of people in
whom evil spirits struggle with the Holy Spirit. They speak of
the Spirit of God coming to dwell with people. Luke's setting
for the Lord's Prayer is an occasion when Jesus was alone with
the disciplines. After speaking with them about petition and
intercession, he says, "If you then, who are evil, know how to
give good gifts to your children, how much more will the
Heavenly Father give the Holy Spirit to those who ask him"
(Luke 11:13).

John's gospel reflects on the Spirit through several discourses. During the conversation with Nicodemus (chap. 3), Jesus says that one must be born of water and the Spirit in order to be indwelt by the Spirit. Speaking to the Samaritan woman by the well, Jesus affirms that God is spirit and those who worship him must worship him in spirit and in truth (John 4:24). At the conclusion of the difficult discourse on the bread of life, Jesus says to his puzzled disciples, "It is the Spirit that gives life; the flesh is of no avail; the words that I have spoken to you are spirit and life" (John 6:63).

What then do the gospels say to us about the spiritual life? They affirm that God is Spirit, and that the human spirit may resist God (as in demon possession) or yearn for God. God is to be worshipped in Spirit and in truth, and we are to be reborn in the Spirit. This Spirit makes it possible for disciples, like their Lord, to preach, heal, and cast out demons. The most moving expression of life in the Spirit comes in John's account of the discourse in the upper room, where Jesus prepared the disciples for his impending death. "If you love me," he says, "you will keep my commandments. And I will pray the Father, and he will give you another Counselor, to be with you forever, even the Spirit of Truth, whom the world cannot receive, because it neither sees him nor knows him; you know him, for he dwells with you, and will be in you" (John 14:15–17). While Jesus was with them, he embodied the reality of God's Holy Spirit. After he left them, the Spirit came among them in a new way: they became Spirit-filled individuals, and together emerged as a spirit-filled community. The double import of Jesus' words must be remembered. As the inheritors of the tradition of Israel, to whom the promise was given that the Spirit would be poured down on the whole community, the disciples would never have interpreted this gift as a personal one given without reference to their special status.

The Acts of the Apostles is the record of a community of faith empowered by the Holy spirit. Stephen's attackers could not resist the Spirit through whom he spoke; thus they instigated his arrest (Acts 6:10). The Spirit sent Philip the evangelist to speak to the Ethiopian (8:29). The Spirit informed Peter that messengers had arrived from Cornelius (10:19), thus initiating his ministry to Gentiles. With the household of Cornelius, the Holy Spirit for the first time fell upon people who were not Jews (11:15). Paul, at one point in his ministry, was prevented by the spirit from speaking in the province of Asia (16:6). In the Spirit he traveled to Macedonia, and "bound in the Spirit" proceeded to Jerusalem, although with a sense of forboding— not knowing what would happen to him there (20:20). The promise of the gospels was fulfilled: the Spirit of God directed the paths of those first evangelists who carried the good news throughout the world they knew.

The letters of Paul are filled with references to the work of the Holy Spirit in the believers and through the church. Paul speaks of the Spirit of Christ dwelling in them; of the power of the Spirit making their work possible. He rejoices in the gift of the Spirit that enables them to heal, to speak boldly, to suffer, and to bring new life. "Do you not know that you are God's temple," he writes, "and that God's Spirit dwells in you?" (1 Cor. 3:16). And later (1 Cor. 12:8) he speaks of the variety of gifts but the same Spirit. Each is given a manifestation of the Spirit for the common good: wisdom, knowledge, faith, healing, miracles, prophecy, speaking in or the interpreting of tongues. These gifts are given not for personal development, but for the strengthening of the Christian community in its work. Here, as elsewhere, the New Testament writers recognize that spirituality is not an interior "feeling" unrelated to God's purposes for all people, but the power to be obedient servants.

The Continuing Development of Spirituality

Observers of the history of spirituality distinguish two forms of the spiritual life. The terms come from the Greek. The *apophatic* technique is one of self-emptying, through which the fullness of God can flow into the seeker. The *kataphatic* technique is imaginal, using mental pictures and words to direct the thoughts toward God. In addition, some methods emphasize an illumination of the mind (the speculative) while other emphasize the warming of the heart (the affective).[1] Each method suits certain people; each expresses the customs of a specific culture or of the spiritual groups developing within a culture. This becomes evident when Christian spirituality is traced beyond the biblical period.

Writings about spirituality are found even during the first few centuries, when there were recurrent periods of persecution: the epistle of Barnabas, the letters of the martyr Ignatius, and the theological writings of Irenaeus. These writers spoke to other Christians about the need for simplicity of life, while at the same time cautioning against ascetical practices of an extreme sort. They acknowledged the spiritual quality of martyrdom, but usually were uncomfortable with the possibility that some people might seek death as a way of canceling all sinfulness. Among the scholars centered in the school at Alexandria during the third and fourth centuries there developed an increasing emphasis on the ascetic life. They believed that the use of reason could help people to detach themselves from the ordinary realities of human existence, such as marriage, in order to concentrate on "the things which are of God." Clement and Origen, his successor as head of the Academy, both preached and practiced this viewpoint. When illumination has been reached, Clement wrote, the soul is purged of human desires and can more completely apprehend God. A hidden knowledge will then be revealed, and scriptures will unfold hidden meanings not known to other readers. Clearly, this approach was for dedicated people who were highly educated, disciplined, and willing, singlemindedly, to practice a life set apart from normative existence. For Clement, Christ alone is the Educator in this Way.

> The self-same Word who forcibly draws men from their natural, worldly way of life, and educates them to the only true salvation: faith in God. That is to say, the heavenly Guide, the Word, once He

begins to call men to salvation, takes it to Himself the name of persuasion . . . instilling in a receptive mind the desire for life now and for the life to come; but the Word also heals and counsels, all at the same time. In fact, He follows up His own activity, by encouraging the one He has already persuaded, and particularly by offering a cure for his passions.[2]

Some people fled to the desert during times of persecution, hoping through a life of deprivation to attain a vision of God. Less intellectual than the Alexandrians, they approached meditation through the words and images of scripture, seeking continued progress, as on a ladder toward perfection. Some, called anchorites, lived in total solitude. Others, called cenobites, lived in communities. In their aloneness, they struggled continually against apathy and listlessness, which could prevent their continuing quest for the vision they had first sought by retiring to the desert.

In west central Turkey, even today marked by few towns, there is an area distinguished by caves and strange natural forms called dolomites. In the fourth century a small group of friends, persons with brilliant speculative minds, came to live here. They sought spiritual perfection through emptying their lives of all material desires. They included the brothers Basil of Caesarea, Gregory of Nyssa, a legislator, and Basil of Nazianzen, a poet and close friend of Basil of Caesarea. Gregory was the spiritual leader of the group. His approach to spirituality began with what he described as an inward drive for oneness with God. Gregory believed this to be a true marriage. Struggling in an ascent from darkness toward the light, a person could strive toward perfection by disciplined living and devotion to God. The goal is never fully achieved, but a continuous growth in goodness is possible. These Cappadocians combined an intense love for God with a rational approach as to how one achieves union with God and an ascetical lifestyle that was only possible for extremely dedicated people.

The writings of Gregory of Nyssa have been deeply influential in the development of Eastern Christian spirituality. He speaks of *synergy*, through which human love (*eros*) directed toward God is interpenetrated by the divine love (*agape*) to form a union with God. This synergy is possible through *hesychia*, which is both the awakening of the soul to God's action and an inner peace, which is the gift of God. Mystics direct their lives toward this goal. Commenting on Moses' vision of God, Gregory writes:

> If nothing comes from above to hinder its upward thrust (for the nature of the Good attracts to itself those who look to it), the soul rises and will always make its flight yet higher—by its desire of the heavenly things *straining ahead for what is to come*, as the Apostle says. \
>
> Made to desire and not to abandon the transcendent height by the things already attained, it makes its way upward without ceasing, ever through its prior accomplishments renewing its intensity for the flight. Activity directed toward virtue causes its capacity to grow through exertion; this kind of activity alone does not slacken its intensity by the effort, but increases it.[3]

The image of Eastern mysticism continued to be that of the light or the process of illumination. The method for coming into the light was through constant prayer. This method has been preserved through the tradition of the Jesus Prayer, which dates from perhaps the sixth century in Egypt. To some late twentieth-century Westerners, this may seem like the "vain repetition" noted in the gospels. To the devout, it may be a deeply devotional experience. Meditation on each word exposes individual meanings. Meditation on each phrase enlarges another set of images: "Lord Jesus Christ"; "Son of God"; "have mercy on me." Finally, the prayer as a whole evokes power as a cry to God.

Words and images are not the total content of the Jesus Prayer. Those who use it constantly find that the words merge until there are no individual sounds but simply an awareness of being deeply into the presence of God. The mood of the prayer seems to be one of petition: "have mercy"; but the emotion generated by the *kyrie* has always been one of adoration.

Hence the one who prays in these words is caught up in a movement from words to wordlessness, from petition to adoration, from self-consciousness (have mercy on *me*) to God-consciousness. The biblical background for the Jesus Prayer is the admonition to "pray without ceasing." Only a limited number of monastics have taken this literally, and the Eastern anchorites certainly have done so.

The concluding name in the list of masters of Eastern spirituality is Dionysius, possibly a Syrian anchorite who lived during the fifth century. He wrote that the ascent of the soul toward God, and the sense of mystery (that is, the human inability to know God) lead to the process of divinization. When the mind of a person becomes infused with the mind or Spirit of God, that person becomes like God; that is, divinized. This does not mean that a human being *becomes* God, or ceases to be human. It means that a person will be completely filled with the divine Spirit acting through the human spirit.

Western Christians are likely to have been influenced in their spiritual quest by Aurelius Augustine. His *Confessions* have been read by many who have found in his struggles a parallel to their own. Reared by a Christian mother, he rejected the claims of Christian commitment until well into adulthood. One day, he writes in this autobiography, struggling against the call of Christ, he heard a voice say, "Take and read." He picked up a book lying on a nearby table and read Paul's words to the Romans that we are justified by faith. Yielding, he renounced his earlier efforts at self-help and in time became the church's staunchest opponent of Pelagius, the man who insisted upon a recognition of personal effort in the work of salvation. Augustine's own continuing struggle was, as he writes, against sensual pleasures, and his ascetic life developed around renouncing love of the world for the love of God as expressed in works of lovingkindness. Augustine writes:

> I looked back on other things and saw that they owe Thee the fact of their existence, and that all things are bounded within Thee, but differently—not as if in a place; rather, because Thou art holding

all with the hand of Truth. All things are true, in so far as they exist, nor is there any falsity, unless when one think something to be which does not exist.[4]

Western Spirituality

Urban T. Holmes, in his survey of Christian spirituality, points to Gregory the Great (540–604) as the father of Western spirituality. The imagery Gregory uses to describe this is "the vision of God" and a vision of light. Contemplation becomes an act of seeing. Holmes writes,

> It appears that where Eastern mysticism, which is a more feminine spirituality, focuses on the receptive heart (the *apophatic*), Western mysticism, which is more masculine, focuses on the action of the eyes (*kataphatic*). We strive for the vision of God—what the late bishop of Oxford, Kenneth Kirk (1886–1954) called the *summum bonum*, the highest good, in his classic work *The Vision of God*. Gregory's asceticism is expressed as a life of servitude. Humility is a virtue. Purity of heart is to see in the center of the self the judgments of God, and to strive for repentance, humility, and patience.[5]

During the Middle Ages, Christianity spread throughout pagan Europe with the inevitable clash of spiritual forms as one religion superseded another. The monasteries were centers for Christian learning and practice. The common people looked for concrete religious practices. Sometimes this was accomplished when earlier religious forms took on a Christian veneer. The hymn popularly known as St. Patrick's Breastplate comes out of early Celtic Christianity and expresses a strong sense of struggle against evil powers: "I bind unto myself the Name, the strong Name of the Trinity."

Medieval society had three segments: clergy, members of religious orders, and laity. The monks were fed spiritually by the liturgy and the offices—the Psalms being an important component of the latter. The laity looked for specific verbal helps in developing their spiritual life: prayers such as the Our Father, the Hail Mary, or the Gloria Patri.

By the apex of this period (1000–1300), the number of monastic foundations had increased, and the Benedictines had been reformed by augmenting community prayer with more emphasis on personal prayer. A trend toward the reclusive life (solitary living) became institutionalized by the Carthusians, who lived in a community but spent their conventual hours in individual cells, gathering only for worship.

Bernard of Clairvaux established the Cistercian order for contemplatives. These monks, like the Carthusians, spent most of their time in personal contemplation, but gathered for meals as well as for common hours of worship. Bernard's writings are classics of spirituality. Deeply imbued with scripture, his meditations focus on the love of God as mediated through Jesus. This devotion to Jesus has been a continuing expression of Western spirituality. He writes:

> The faithful soul sighs deeply for his presence, rests peacefully when thinking of him, and must glory in the degradation of the Cross until it is capable of contemplating the glory of God's revealed face. Thus Christ's bride and dove pauses for a little and rests amidst her inheritance after receiving by lot, from the memory of your abundant sweetness, Lord Jesus, silver-tinted wings, the candor of innocence and purity, and she hopes to be filled with gladness at the sight of your face. . . .[6]

Members of the order established by Francis of Assisi (1181–1226) were called "friars" because they worked among people, as distinguished from monks who lived and worked only within the monasteries. Franciscans went among the people to preach and do good works. Franciscan piety was devoted to the crucified Christ, with whom Francis himself became identified to the point of experiencing the stigmata, the wounds of Christ. Poverty and simplicity of life were basic to their practice.

Another order of friars established at this period, the Dominicans, also ministered to people outside the monastery. Preaching was their work. Popular piety found expression in devotion to the Holy Name, the Blessed Sacrament, and the Sacred

Heart. Devotion to the Virgin Mary increased in popularity, encouraging a feminine element of piety. It was felt that the Mother of Jesus could understand the sufferings of human beings because of her own suffering. This is different from the liturgical piety of Eastern Orthodoxy centered in the Theotokos, Mother of God, whose icon is revered but whose role has been strictly defined within her relationship to the Incarnation. In late medieval Western Christianity, Mary the Mother became a comforting and sustaining figure.

Among the best-known devotional writings are those written during the late Middle Ages. Meister Eckhart (1260–1327) writes of the ineffability and incomprehensibility of God. The seeker enters into a darkness of unknowing, yet there is a spark of God that can illuminate the soul and bring a sense of oneness with God. Eckhart, like others among the mystics, seems sometimes to blur the fine line between pantheism (God is part of all creation) and the biblical understanding of the self-identity of God apart from, yet related to, the created world. John Tauler (1300–1361) urges on his readers repentance, good works, and the cultivation of the peace of God.

The earliest of the fourteenth-century English mystics is Richard Rolle (c. 1295–1349), who writes about the fire of love, that intense mystical love of God experienced by the contemplative. *The Cloud of Unknowing*, by an unknown priest, affirms that in experiencing ourselves and drawing near to God we know God (and do not need to know *about* God). The title takes its name from an early section of the book:

> For when you first begin to undertake it (the exercise of concentrating on God alone), all that you find is a darkness, a sort of cloud of unknowing; you cannot tell what it is, except that you experience in your will a simple reaching out to God. This darkness and cloud is always between you and your God, no matter what you do, and it prevents you from seeing him clearly by the light of understanding in your reason, and from experiencing him in sweetness of love in your affection. So set yourself to rest in this darkness as long as you can, always crying out after him whom you love. For if you are to

experience him or to see him at all, insofar as it is possible here, it must always be in this cloud and in this darkness. So if you labour at it with all your attention as I bid you, I trust, in his mercy, that you will reach this point.[7]

Julian of Norwich fixes her devotion on the person of the crucified Christ. The Eucharist is central to her life, and this binds her to the church. Jesus Christ is our true Mother, she writes, and affirms that he will raise us up in the fullness of his life. Julian, it will be recalled, was the spiritual director of Margery Kempe, in whose own writing much use is made of spiritual visions.

Contemplation through the mystical way reached its height during this period. It is interesting to note the pattern on which this spirituality was built. The approach to God began with an act of purgation. Anyone who desired to draw near to the Holy One needed to be emptied of all sin, evil, human desires, and anything else that might stand between the self and an awareness of the divine. When that was accomplished, a person began the process of illumination. God began to be revealed. The person whose love for God was now purified was enabled to apprehend and respond to the divine love. Years of intense waiting upon God, oblivious of personal desire, brought an ever-deepened sense of illumination. The figures of "light" and "brightness" come to mind from the writings of the Cappadocians. Finally, there is the stage of union, in which the soul is united in love with God. This is not to be identified with the idea of absorption into the All which is a feature of Eastern (Hindu) mysticism or of pantheism. The figure the mystics used is that of marriage, of the union and absorption of lover and beloved. Some, like Teresa of Avila, are explicit in their descriptions of the divine union in terms of sexual union. In this union there is complete surrender, and at the same time an awareness of separateness. God is God and the contemplative is still human.

There is also a technical vocabulary of prayer. *Meditation* is a technique in which words and images (frequently from the Bible) form a basis for thoughts from which the mind seeks to deepen the understanding of God, the relationship to God, and a cultivation of love for God. *Contemplation* is the next step. A person goes beyond words and images, even beyond thoughts, to "feel" the presence of God. In human terms, contemplation expresses the idea that love cannot be adequately conveyed in words, or even actions. One has, at best, a deep inner awareness of the power and fullness of love. This is how the contemplative seeks to deepen relationship to God. *Mental prayer* is a third form: prayer expressed in words. The Our Father or any other written form is mental prayer. Also, the spontaneous words in which people express to God their thanksgiving and petition are forms of mental prayer. Some people have found that they can pray only in learned forms. Others have prayed only in their own words. Both forms have a place in the development of the spiritual life.

Forms of Modern Spirituality

Three powerful examples of the spiritual life come from fifteenth-century Spain during the time of the Reformation in northern Europe and the Counter-Reformation (including the Inquisition) in Spain. One is Teresa of Avila, who reformed the Carmelite order and became a model for the energetic, managerial sort of person who could also practice a deep spirituality. How she had time for both is a mystery to most people, as well as how the same person could engage so fully in what seem, to the modern mind, like disparate lifestyles—being both active and contemplative. Teresa writes:

> It also seems to me that His Majesty is testing to see who it is who loves Him: He tests now this one, now another, by revealing who He is with a superb delight and by quickening faith—if it is dead—in what He will give us, saying, "Look, this is but a drop from the vast sea of blessings." He does this so as to leave nothing undone

for those who love Him; in the measure He sees that they receive Him, so He gives and is given. He loves whoever loves Him: how good a beloved![8]

John of the Cross, her spiritual director, has been instructive to many seekers by his description of the "dark night of the soul" (spirit)—that tunnel through which everyone passes during gestation of the spiritual life. There comes a period in which the senses are dark and the mind does not understand spiritual things. Then comes a darkness of the spirit in which one feels alienated from God. Finally, through the darkness comes illumination.

Ignatius of Loyola founded the Society of Jesus as an organization through which Europe might be won back to its Catholic Christian faith. The members were to be disciplined the way an army is, willing to go wherever they were sent. They became the first modern missionaries—well-trained, well-educated couriers who took the gospel to China and Japan, fulfilling an apologetic task even more than an evangelistic one. They won respect because of their ability to appreciate other cultures. Ignatius' *Spiritual Exercises,* written for the members of his order, have found new popularity today as a method of meditation. Reading a passage of scripture, one imagines the scene, places the self there, responds to the Lord, and prays to be enabled to love and follow him.

Anglican spirituality can be appreciated through the writings of John Donne (especially his poetry), Lancelot Andrewes, and Jeremy Taylor. These are not monastics, but people "in the world." Their spirituality is rooted in the eucharistic liturgy and in incarnational theology.

A classical approach to the spiritual life was recovered in a new way by the Society of Friends, the Quakers, and first expressed through the writings of George Fox. Their emphasis was on waiting upon the Spirit, on seeking the guidance of the Inner Light. Their congregational worship, in a simple meetinghouse, consists of waiting in silence until the Holy Spirit guides a member to offer prayer, scripture, or sermon. Theirs is the nearest approach within the Protestant tradition to an affirmation of the monastic cultivation of the spiritual life through silence. Fox wrote in his diary:

> Sept. 10: Longed with intense desire after God; my whole soul seemed impatient to be conformed to him, and to become "holy, as he is holy." In the afternoon, prayed with a dear friend privately, and had the presence of God with us; our souls united together to reach after a blessed immortality, to be unclosed of the body of sin and death, to enter the blessed world, where no unclean things enter. O, with what intense desire did our souls long for that blessed day, that we might be freed from sin, and for ever lived to and in our God! . . . Blessed be God for every such divine gale of his Spirit, to speed me on in my way to the new Jerusalem.[9]

John Woolman, an early American exemplar, also recorded a now-famous *Journal*. More recent writers in this tradition have included American authors such as Rufus M. Jones, Thomas Kelly, and Douglas Steere.

There is another, and less exemplary, strain in modern spirituality: the pietistic. This is at times a sentimentalizing of piety, and becomes an exaggeration of classical devotional emphases. Within Roman Catholicism, some devotions to the Virgin Mary, the Sacred Heart, and the Reserved Sacrament had become pietistic, until reformed after Vatican II. Among Protestants, such piety has sometimes been referred to as "Jesus-olatry," an emphasis on the humanity of Jesus that may be comforting to people who need identification with him in their suffering, but which robs their spirituality of the strength that is to be found in the biblical sense of awe at the Incarnation, Passion, and Resurrection of the Lord. Blaise Pascal (1623–1662), bordered on pietism. Recall his much-quoted "The heart has reasons of which reason knows not." One implication of the statement (Pascal was a mathematician and presumably a "hard" thinker) could be that reason is not a necessary component of the religious life. Pascal's writing centers on the personal aspects of salvation. This will be recognized as an important component of much Protestant pietism, particularly as expressed in nineteenth-century hymnody, not only in Lutheran Germany, but in American free church revivalism.

John Wesley, influenced by the Moravians, but also by classical piety, preached to large crowds the good news of the sanctifying influence of the Holy Spirit on personal living. He was protesting the aridity of the established church. Wesley affirmed the possibility of Christian perfection but was not specific about its probability. He sought to restore to the church the warmth inherent in the practice of faith. The Wesleyan tradition has been faithful when it cultivated its theological/ biblical roots, but has sometimes wandered into a sentimental piety. The American religious spirit has sometimes been neglectful, even disparaging, of theological roots, and then has had no norms from which to differentiate between piety as expressive of biblical faith and that which grows out of a cultural mood.

Who are the spiritual guides today? Certainly one would name such persons as Dag Hammarskjöld, Simone Weil, Martin Luther King, Jr., and Thomas Merton. One would want to add, from the Jewish tradition, Martin Buber and Abraham Heschel—but of them more later.

Learning About the Spiritual Way

To be educated for the spiritual life involves more than simply reading about spirituality in the Bible or in writings from the continuing Christian tradition. Nevertheless, these are the places at which to begin. We are not the originators of Christian spirituality. Excesses of pietism come from personal belief in a new revelation of God quite apart from the ways in which God has been revealed through the generations. To learn about the spiritual life is to identify with those who have struggled, learned, and practiced it. Sometimes their lives parallel our own; sometimes they seem far different in time, culture, or the circumstances of their being. At other times their spiritual experiences seem not at all to be dependent upon sociological settings. We are one in the Spirit, and empathy is generated as we recognize in the writing of someone who lived long ago a need similar to our own. All people have times of sorrow and of joy; know times when they can pray and times when God seems far distant; are filled with thanksgiving or long most of all to plead their desperate need. Those who spent a lifetime cultivating the spiritual life may have put into concrete expression thoughts, ideas, and insights that we have dimly grasped but have not known how to articulate. Such writings help to concretize the personal journey in faith. The writer's story becomes our story: we are one with Augustine, Gregory, Julian, Fox, and King.

We also learn about growth in the spiritual life as we are able to view each individual in the story as a specific person. It is helpful to learn about the range of Christian spirituality through a survey, even as brief a one as this chapter has offered. But that is only a beginning. The reader needs to choose from this story a few people who could be exemplars. Who seemed to express your spiritual need as you read? Choose one person and look up one writing, or a brief compilation of that person's writings. Get to know that person by reading a biography. Even the brief entry in an encyclopedia will give some factual background, orienting the person in time and place. A more complete biography is written by someone who cared enough to delve into a life, and the resulting volume gives the reader the possibility of "feeling into" the life of the other. To become seriously interested in education for the spiritual life, a person needs to discover biographical materials that are honest, sympathetic, and informative.

Reading about a person is one dimension for knowing a person. Autobiography can provide a more personal dimension than biography. In any event, it is essential that one read the writings in order to share in a spiritual journey as another is willing to share it. Some writings are difficult; others seem archaic. The best approach may be to start with excerpts: an anthology of writings from one person, or a collection that includes the writings of a number of people. Current interest in the subject has brought about the publication in recent years of a number of well-edited anthologies, and a number of beautifully illustrated collections of excerpts have been compiled.[10] While these do not bring one deeply into the thought of a person like Teresa or John of the Cross, they give one some food for meditation. This is a good beginning. If one feels a kinship with the writer, one can always find more complete collections to provide material for serious study. It is in studying as well as in reading meditatively that we grow in the spiritual life.

Subsequently, one will want to practice the methods developed by these people. Several offer deliberately planned ways of meditation for those under their care. Ignatius has five methods, ranging from one for the illiterate to the full Ignatian method. The Sulpicians also had a method of meditation. As was noted earlier, the Jesus Prayer is used by some people today. No method should be followed in a mechanical way, but in a manner that will free one for an ever-deepening awareness of the Presence of God, while at the same time relating to everyday life. Silence is the basis for the congregational worship of Friends, but its use in contemplation and meditation is an essential element in any life of prayer. It is not easy to practice silence; for some people silence may seem uncomfortable. It begins with a period of deliberately designed relaxation, followed by an entrance into silence through word or picture images. At first the time spent in silence will probably be brief, but gradually this time will be lengthened. In the busyness of contemporary life, even taking time for quietness may seem like an intrusion until we learn to experience the joy of it.

Finally, one can learn about the spiritual life through people who have been practicing it for a number of years, and from pelple who are at various stages along the way. Every congregation will include a few such persons—and they are as likely to be laity as clergy. Such "exemplars" of spirituality do not usually talk much about their spiritual life. One may be attracted to them by an awareness of their serenity. Through casual conversation we may just happen to realize that they and we are both reading similar books, and may be engaged in a similar quest. One may find this other person in a group to which one belongs. Sometimes small prayer or spiritual life groups form because a few people sense that they can be mutually supportive. They will discover the particular gifts that each brings to the group as well as their individual needs.

One important factor in the search for other seekers is that in a new way we become aware of the continuities in the development of the spiritual life. As there were Spirit-filled people in the Bible and throughout succeeding centuries, so the Holy Spirit is still at work in and through people whose lives are witnesses to the gracious love of God. As in biblical times, so today the Spirit works through those who are consciously committed to being part of the Christian community, "the blessed company of all faithful people."

4. Learning from One Another

Religious traditions differ from one another in many ways: beliefs, forms of worship, even some prescriptions for living. Each has a separate history. However, they share one aspect in common: the yearning for a deeper knowledge of and relationship to God.

The Quest in Judaism

The quest of the Jewish people is first documented in the Hebrew Bible, but the quest did not end there. A psalmist wrote, "Oh, how I love thy law! It is my meditation all the day. . . . How sweet are thy words to my taste, sweeter than honey to my mouth" (Ps. 119:97, 103). But in the first centuries of the Common Era, the Law became, for many people, a burden rather than a delight. Its precepts became so narrowly hedged with interpretations that only the learned could understand and only people who had leisure could hope to observe them faithfully. Later, difficulties arose from exile in the alien cultures of Europe and increasing persecution. Many Jews in Spain, Eastern Europe, and the Ottoman Empire yearned for a more personal relationship to God. The continuing hope of the coming of Messiah seemed frustrated. Redemption had never seemed farther away.

As if in answer to this need, the Kabbalah developed during the early thirteenth century in Catalonia and Provence. Kabbalah is a word that denotes mystical writings, and these were contained in the *Safer ha Zohar*, or *Book of Splendor*, usually shortened to *Zohar*. This collection was first printed in 1558.

The writer was Moses de Leon, who lived in Provence. The Kabbalah referred to a series of ten steps (*sleevor*) through which the believer ascended into the fullness of the revelation of God. The first, or lowest, step was that of the *Shekinah*, the divine presence. Above the *Shekinah*, the steps ascended to the foundation of all the powers active in God: the majesty, eternity, beauty, might, love, intelligence, and wisdom up to the Supreme Crown. Redemption, the Kabbalah asserted, would come through the reunion of the *Shekinah* to the other spheres. The integration of prayer, praxis, and belief would eventually bring harmony.[1]

Isaak Luria (1534–1572) was born in Jerusalem and died at Safed. He wrote little, but his thought was transmitted through his disciples and became known as the Lurianic Kabbalah. These teachings spread through the Ottomon Empire and into Poland. Rabbi Shabbetai Tzevi of Smyrna (1626–1676), living in a time of persecution, declared himself Messiah in 1665. Although his was a short-lived reign (he was forcibly converted to Islam within a year), he attracted followers and a new sect developed.

The modern Hasidic movement dates from the time of Israel ben Eliezar (1700–1760), known as the Ba'al Shem Tov (meaning Master of the Good Name), who lived in Poland. The significance of his name lies in the popular belief that he possessed the secret of the name of God, and that this enabled him to be a healer.

Judaism has preserved the tradition earlier cited from the psalmist of experiencing the love of God through faithfully seeking to interpret Torah and live its precepts through *Mizvot*, or good works. Such ardent study was life to scholars, but to ordinary people, beset by poverty and persecution, study was not possible. They yearned for a more immediate assurance that the Lord was with them in their suffering. This way of inner certainty expounded by the Ba'al was appealing. The word "Hasidic" means "pious," and the term later became attached to the movement itself as one made up of pious people.

Other leaders who seemed to have this sense of the immediacy of the divine Presence showed a charismatic quality that attracted followers. Today, Hasidic congregations still form around a *Zadik* ("righteous leader"), or the *Reebe* ("rabbi"), and his son becomes designated inheritor of the charism.

In common with members of other mystical traditions, the Hasidim are imbued with a sense of wonder over the creative work of God. The fact that creation occurred by virtue of the divine Word established the foundation for the meaning of the Kabbalah, the mystical *Words*. The affirmation of God's Presence in all creation underlies the Hasidic belief in the personal nearness of God. In seeking the divine Presence, the believer holds in tension both love and fear toward God: fear, because God is the ineffable, transcendent Holy One; love because God is also the Creator and Redeemer, the source of all life. Worship and personal devotional practices cultivate this two-pronged awareness.

One Hasidic writer says:

As a person begins his prayer, reciting the words:

> O Lord, open my lips
> and let my mouth declare Your praise,
> the Presence of God comes into him.

Then it is the Presence herself

> who commands his voice:
> it is she who speaks the words *through* him.

One who knows in faith

> that all this happens within him
> will be overcome with trembling
> and with awe.[2]

Members of Hasidic groups may be recognized today by their distinctive dress. They are faithful in studying Torah and seem to interpret with a rigidity more reminiscent of the learned rabbis from which they first dissented. But there is also a spontaneity in worship. They are distinguished by their ecstatic dance and utterance on festival occasions.[3]

This personal approach to the understanding of God has been introduced to a wide audience through the writings of Martin Buber, the theologian whose book *I and Thou* has been influential among Christians as well as Jews. Buber makes a distinction between the relationship that people properly have with objects as an I-it relationship, and the relationship with another human being as an I-Thou one. These relationships should be personal and subjective. To treat persons as objects is to fail to recognize the special quality of being human. Objective knowledge about a person (the resumé or "vita") is one source of knowledge, but this source is made complete by a knowledge of God, speaking *about* God's love, wisdom, and power. The believer knows God through a different dimension (just as God knows the believer): in a relationship of love and awe toward the Holy One. Buber writes:

> In the relation to God, unconditional exclusiveness and unconditional inclusiveness are one. For those who enter into the absolute relationship, nothing particular retains any importance—neither things nor beings, neither earth nor heaven—but everything is included in the relationship. For entering into the pure relationship does not involve ignoring everything but seeing everything in the You, not renouncing the world but placing it upon its proper ground. Looking away from the world is no help toward God; staring at the world is no help either; but whoever beholds the world in him stands in his presence. World here, God there—that is it-Talk; and God in the world—that, too, is it-Talk; but leaving out nothing, leaving nothing behind, to comprehend all—all the world—in comprehending the You, giving the world its due and truth, to have nothing besides God but to grasp everything in him, that is the perfect relationship.[4]

Another modern interpreter of the personal understanding of God is the late Abraham J. Heschel, professor at Jewish Theological Seminary in New York. He writes:

> Prayer is like the light from a burning glass in which all the rays that emanate from the soul are gathered to a focus. There are hours when we are resplendent with the glowing awareness of our share

in His secret interest on earth. We pray. We are carried forward in Him who is coming close to us. We endeavor to divine His will, not merely His command. Prayer is an answer to God: "Here am I."[5]

Christians and Jews share common roots in the Bible. Al though two separate traditions emerged, whenever their spirituality is informed by a return to this heritage, each helps the other in the quest. Thus the Hasidic writings, the philosophical insights of Martin Buber, and the meditative words of Abraham Heschel are lights along the path.

Islamic Spirituality

Of the three religions that arose in the Middle East on a foundation of faith in One God, Islam was the latest to emerge. The founder, the Prophet Muhammad (570–632), was born and died at Mecca. Bringing a faith in one God to the people of Arabia, he left them with Holy Scriptures, the Qur'ān and a religion based on the five "Pillars of Islam." There are (1) the profession of faith: "There is no god but Allah, and Muhammad is his prophet"; (2) the prayers recited five times daily; (3) charitable giving: (4) fasting (during the month of Ramadan), and (5) the pilgrimage to the holy city of Mecca.

This is a concrete expression of religious living with wide appeal. It could also become legalistic, leaving in some believers the yearning for a more personal approach to God.

Islamic mysticism first arose as an ascetic movement, in protest to the worldliness that developed soon after Muhammad's time (the Unayyad period, 661–749). Small brotherhoods formed, gathering to meditate on the Qur'ān. They tried faithfully to fulfill its precepts and were noted for their piety. The second reason for the development of Islamic mysticism was the yearning for a deeper personal relationship to God. This expression is first ascribed to Rabiah al-Adawiyah (d. 801) from Sasra. Writing in poetry, the primary vehicle for Islamic mysticism, she proclaimed an ideal love for God that was free from both the hope of heaven and the fear of hell. This theme appears later in Christian writings and it is probable that Christian hermits of that period were exchanging ideas with Islamic ascetics.

As devotional writing, a work second only to the Qur'ān itself is the long poem *Masnavi* by Jalal ad-Din ar Rumi (1207–1273). He is renowned as the inspiration for the mystical brotherhood known as the whirling dervishes. Sufi meditation draws inspiration from the Qur'ān as do other Moslems when they meditate on the love of God. They strive for an understanding of God which goes beyond the law, however beneficent it may be, into the reality of God, who is both within the world and transcendent. Sufis are brotherhoods, not monastic orders. Each member works and has a family, but they reinforce one another in their spiritual life through the common discipline they share. Not many people adopt this lifestyle, but the Sufis have been influential in the development of a form of spirituality.

To the transcendent affirmation that Allah the Merciful is One, and that life consists in submission to the divine will ("Islam" means "submission"), the Sufis add that God loves, and humans can live in a state of reciprocal love with God. The phrase "God loves" relates to the divine existence, and includes the ineffability of the Divine Being. The Arabic words of the basic confession, with their rhythm and repetition, form a mantra when repeated continually in love and wonder: *La ilaha illa Alla*—"there is no god but God."

In their writing, Sufis used the symbol of light. They speak of the yearning of the soul for union with God. Like mystics in other traditions, they seek a reality beyond the mundane; an absolute Goodness and Truth beyond human fallibility; a fullness of selfhood that leads them beyond self. They seek to become one with God while always knowing that God has an existence separate from the rest of creation. In Kenneth Cragg's collection *The Wisdom of the Sufis*, there are some choice examples, such as these:

XXII

Perfect, perfect, perfect,	Holy, Holy, Holy
Thrice perfect is this love:	Thrice holy is this light,
Empty, empty, empty	Meeting, meeting, meeting,
This flesh and the lusts	Today with the Infinite.[6]
thereof.	

CXXXI

I thought I had arrived at the very Throne of God and said to it: "O Throne, they tell us that God rests upon thee." "O Bayazid" replied the Throne, "We are told here that He dwells in a humble heart."[7]

Eastern Religions

Despite references to the "mysterious East," contacts between Europe and Asia go back through many centuries. Alexander the Great led his army as far east as India. Christian tradition places the establishment of the church there on the activity of Thomas the apostle, for whom one body of it is named Mar Thoma. Nestorian Christians from the Middle East, accused of heresy and exiled from their churches, carried the gospel into China. Those early Christian congregation disappeared, but Christians again entered that country in the sixteenth century with Francis Xavier and other Jesuits. By that time, the silk route had long been established, bearing caravans of goods for trade from China to Europe. Cultural exchange was inevitable.

Buddhism arose in India. Siddhartha Gautama, the Buddha (a title of reverence meaning "the Enlightened One") lived in northern India, gathered his disciples there, and gave them the *Dhamma* ("the Truth"), the middle path that leads to vision and knowledge and ultimately to Nirvana. The four "Noble Truths" are: (1) Existence is full of conflict, desire, sorrow, and suffering; (2) All this is caused by selfish desire; (3) There is liberation: Nirvana; (4) The way to liberation through the "Noble Eightfold Path" is: right view, right thought, right speech, right action, right mode of living, right endeavor, right mindfulness, and right concentration.

Buddhism began as an ascetic movement. Gautama, the Buddha, left his loved wife and infant son at the call to seek Enlightenment and gathered a group of disciples. The monastic discipline of his followers, from novice to professed monk or nun, parallels that of Christian monastic groups.

In keeping with the basic doctrine of the Buddha, the goal of the mystic is not absorption into the Divine, but a freeing of the self from the bonds of existence. Enlightenment is to *know* the illusory quality of human existence. This is a human enterprise through which a person following the Noble Eightfold path frees the self from desire and achieves Nirvana (liberation). The goal of concentration is the integration of the self.

Several methods for achieving the goal have become widely known and practiced among nonreligious people as techniques of relaxation, a way of promoting well-being and renewing energy. They have attracted the interest of those Christians who can feel kinship with others seeking deepened spiritual awareness.

One such practice is that of Yoga. Yoga is a discipline for quieting the body. The first step is the position taken: seated at ground level, legs bent at the knee with feet tucked under them, arms crossed or lying lightly on the knees. Breathing exercises that monitor inhaling and exhaling at regular intervals are integral to both the posture of the body and its balance. Thus used, this is not just a form of relaxation, but a deliberate concentration on the body in a particular way in order to bring it under control for meditation.[8]

The mantra (or *koan*, in Japanese) is another Buddhist practice. This is a secret saying given the novice by the retreat master. By concentrating on this brief thought at length, the one who meditates achieves both inner tranquility and deepened awareness. Many know the *koan* about silence as the sound of one hand clapping. There is an enigmatic quality to the *koan*, but in its basic technique it has something in common with the Jesus Prayer used in Hesychasm or the Sufi concentration on the affirmation of the Oneness of Allah. A phrase or verse from the Bible, for example, can become a form of *koan*, when given to someone for meditation.

There are three basic forms of Buddhism. Hinayana (the earliest form) predominates in Southeast Asia and Sri Lanka; Mahayana predominates in East Asia; and Tibetan or Tantric Buddhism is found in the Himalayan region. Beatrice Lane Suzuki, whose husband D. T. Suzuki was instrumental in interpreting Buddhism to English-speaking peoples, in her study of Mahayana Buddhism, cites this extract from a Sutra:

> Wisdom grows in three ways: Hearing, Meditating, and Practicing.
>
> Hearing is to love the doctrine which one has learned and never to be weary of it.
>
> Meditating is to meditate on all things as they are, considering them as transient, causing pain, empty, and having no self, whereby to loathe them and walk towards the wisdom of the Buddha.
>
> Practicing is to be separated from desire and evil thought, and by degrees to enter the way of Enlightenment.[9]

These meditational practices are important to Zen Buddhism, which was brought to China in the sixth century by a South Indian monk. It was introduced into Japan in the seventh century, but developed slowly until the twelfth century. Zen has influenced the martial arts, the No drama, flower arrangement, and the tea ceremony—all of which are artistic expressions of a highly disciplined ritual.

Zen Buddhism has had a following among Europeans, Americans, and Canadians during the last decades of the twentieth century. Meditational practices have been found helpful by Christians seeking ways of deepening the spiritual life. This interaction between two faiths, finding unity in forms while drawing from different content to meet their needs, enlarges ecumenical frontiers. The openness resulting from Vatican II goes beyond any attempts at synthesis. People of each tradition are able to learn from the other, as well as to share their common quest.

Hinduism is the religion of millions who inhabit the subcontinent of India. It is the soil out of which Buddhism grew. Syncretistic at the core, the Hindu is open to see a manifestation of God (Brahma) in all deities. Travelers to India often are taken to a temple in old Delhi in which there is an altar to Christ among those to other manifestations of the Divine. The ideal of the Brahmin, a man of the upper class (or caste), is to live in three phases: growing up, marrying and raising a family, and then retiring to the contemplative life. Mystical awareness has long been sought in India. The earliest scriptural texts go back as early as 1500–1000 B.C. The development of the spiritual life is derived from the Bhakti mystical tradition, which developed in South India in the ninth and tenth centuries.

For Hinduism the goal of the spiritual life is the release of the self from matter. Control of body and mind is a way of disciplining the self for this freedom. Knowing is being—both intellectual knowing and the awareness that comes through relationship to the Divine. Such knowing has transforming value. Hinduism is a monistic religion; that is, it views God as being an integral part of the created universe, not having a separate existence. Evil is also part of the universe: to become free from its power becomes more important than trying to overcome it, since evil pervades existence.

Later schools personified the godhead in Siva, Vishnu, and his incarnation in Rama and Krishna. This incarnational aspect opened up the possibility of relationship, and, as in other religious traditions, there developed the figure of the soul seeking the Divine Lover.

Today, forms of modern Hinduism have found their way into the Western world. The guru is the teacher who gives the initiate the mantra on which to meditate. Another guru guides the person along the Way (Bhakti). Several Hindu groups have established centers in the United States. The devotional practices from Buddhism outlined previously are similarly characteristic of Hinduism: meditation, Yoga exercises, and the mantra. The

contribution of Hinduism to Christianity has been explored by
Graham Aelrod, who has been participating in Hindu–Roman
Catholic dialogue in recent years.[10]

An earlier rapprochement between the two traditions was
formed through Theosophy, a late-nineteenth-century development whose center today is at Varanasi. The Ramakrishna
movement was a reform in Hinduism designed to adapt it to
societal needs.

Undoubtedly one of the world figures most admired by
Christians is Mohandas K. Gandhi (1869–1948). As a young
man he was influenced by the Sermon on the Mount, but rejected Christianity as a form of faith after he had seen the way
Indians in South Africa were treated by Christians. His doctrine of nonviolent protest depended for its efficacy upon a
deeply disciplined spiritual life. Gandhi's was a spiritual life
turned outward. He did not view freedom in the classical Hindu
sense as liberation from the illusory world. He preferred to
transform the world into a place where people might live in
mutual peacefulness and cooperation. The ashram, a gathering
of people around a spiritual leader for the purposes of deepening the spiritual life, attracted Westerners, who took the idea
back and established such spiritual centers in other countries.
It is a form of retreat center.

Christians are becoming aware that the original religion of
the Native Americans was also a quest for a deepened spirituality. They were cognizant of the action of God in creation and of
the relationship of humans to the rest of the created order. In
Africa, now turning from its ancient faith toward the newer
religions of Islam and Christianity, there has been the ever-
present sense that all of life is a gift of the Eternal. Theologian
John Mbiti has collected some of the prayers of his people.
This one is from Kenya:

> O, my Father, great Elder, I have no words to thank you, but with
> your deep widsom I am sure that you can see how much I prize
> your glorious gifts. O my Father, when I look upon your greatness I

am confounded with awe. O great Elder, ruler of all things both on heaven and on earth, I am your warrior, I am ready to act in accordance with your will.[11]

Other Forms of Spirituality

So pervasive is the need for a sense of harmony with the universe, of relaxation from tension, and of inner quiet as a basis for renewal, that it is no wonder people without religious faith seek forms of spirituality. "Spiritual" in this sense becomes a quality of the human person to be cultivated as an integral part of life. Transcendental Meditation (TM), with roots in Hinduism, is practiced by people for whom the form itself gives inner meaning. The half hour of meditation, using a mantra, at the opening and close of day, gives them, they testify, a sense of power that enables them to increase their workload and not tire. Transcendental Meditation was introduced into the United States in 1957 by Maharishi Mahesh Yogi.[12] Est, Werner Erhard's technique, builds on a method of helping people both relax and feel renewed.

Recently, Christian conference and retreat centers have been offering programs on Ira Progoff's techniques of journal-keeping. While it is well-known that literary and religious figures have bared their souls through memoirs (Augustine's *Confessions* being among them), the method of journal-keeping invites anyone who can write to make a conscious effort to recall the past and record the present. The object of this discipline is to bring back memories, especially painful memories that tend to be repressed, to face these fully, and to be able to forgive the self and the other(s) involved in the memory. This is a way of healing the past and bringing wholeness to the present. It is recognized that the spiritual life as relationship to God can only be developed by understanding the relationships among sin, repentance, forgiveness, and restoration. This restoration is on both the human level and on the human/divine level. Only through such action can there come that inner

peace on which rests all growth in the spiritual life. This rationale clearly brings journal-keeping into the realm of spiritual
disciplines.

The Contribution of Others to Spiritual Learning

It must be apparent from this overview that Christian spirituality, rich as it is, cannot neglect the contributions of other
people. This survey indicates that the quest for a deepened
spirituality and a closer relationship to God, however named, is
at the heart of all religious practice. Prayer is an activity among
all peoples; worship and various liturgical forms to suit the experiences of individuals and their groups are an expression of
community life everywhere.

Those who read and consider the stories of the Hasidic masters, with their incisive commentary on the discourse between
God and humans, will find their spiritual life enriched. Buber's
distinctions between I-Thou and I-it, applied both to human
relationships and the approach to God, are thoughtful insights
that cannot be neglected. A lifetime of prayer, encapsulated in
the brief writings of Heschel, is a permanent enrichment for all
who seek to practice spiritual disciplines in the face of the mul-
titudinous distractions of present-day life.

The ecstatic, spontaneous approach of the mystics, whether
Hasidic or Sufi, can raise questions about a modern approach
to religious expression for many Christians still largely trapped
in the cognitive modes bequeathed by the doctrinal Reformation and the eighteenth-century Age of Reason. Many who are
wary of charismatic expressions still need to consider the mystic's yearning to love God, motivated by sheer devotion rather
than fear of judgment or hope of gain.

The study of Eastern and other forms of spirituality offers
techniques that can be appropriated into whatever may be
one's own Western tradition. This has already been demonstrated by some Christians, who have replaced the traditional
picture or Cross on a wall above a table set with candle and/or

Bible by a cushion on the floor before a symbol placed at eye-level when seated. Yoga has taught people a way of preparing the body for devotion. The introduction of the idea of mantra from the East has made Christians newly aware that others also have methods for meditation and helps for spiritual growth. The introduction of Asian forms of spirituality, sometimes in the past viewed apprehensively by Christians as a threat to or a distortion of their own faith, has instead enabled them to rediscover treasures they had forgotten, neglected, or never considered. It has also given them an opportunity, on this small earth, to become aware of certain desires all religious people hold in common, the quests that they share. This in no way compromises the distinctiveness of each, but can instead make uniqueness clearer. Thomas Merton in the introduction to his book *Mysticism and Zen Masters* writes: "There is a wider 'oikoumene' (i.e., beyond the 'household of the faith'), the household and the spiritual family of man seeking the meaning of his life and its ultimate purpose."[13]

5. Conflict and Spiritual Growth

The spiritual life can be a positive factor in human life by assisting people in meeting uncomfortable situations, or it can be a negative factor, helping them to avoid such situations. In order to understand what this means, it will be helpful to look at two terms: objectivity and subjectivity.

The Objective View

Popularly speaking, objectivity is a way of looking at people or events from the outside. It suggests that the viewer stands apart, uninvolved emotionally, analyzing a situation in a totally rational way. Is this possible? Danish philosopher-theologian Søren Kierkegaard ridiculed this idea more than a century ago. We bring ourselves into any evaluation, he said, and this is an immediate source of bias. We cannot escape it. True objectivity is to realize the personal bias, and take this into account. We dare not pretend that the mind makes a decision untainted by other considerations. Kierkegaard recognized three levels of knowledge about God. On the aesthetic level, people think that being religious is a beautiful experience. On the philosophical level, they consider the idea of God to be important. Such people affirm that God exists, but that knowledge does not influence the way they live. God exists outside the world and puts no claims upon it. On the level of theological knowledge, the consideration is not knowledge *about* God but knowledge *of* God. This latter is a knowledge gained through a relationship with God.

The theologian explains faith in cognitive terms, so that people can try to understand intellectually. A theologian might also share the experience of faith, writing in subjective terms. Aurelius Augustine wrote a treatise on the Trinity, and, as mentioned previously, a spiritual autobiography entitled *Confessions*. Thomas Aquinas wrote the *Summa Theologica*. He also wrote hymns that revealed another dimension of faith.

Creeds are affirmations of faith. A person could meditate on one of the sections of the Apostles' Creed. "I believe in God the Father Almighty, Maker of heaven and earth" is a statement of faith.

Martin Luther, in *A Brief Explanation of the Creed*, writes:

> We should note that there are two ways of believing. One way is to believe about God as I do when I believe that what is said of God is true; just as I do when I believe what is said about the Turk, the devil, or hell. This faith is knowledge or observation rather than faith. The other way is to believe in God, as I do when I not only believe that what is said about Him is true, but put my trust in Him; surrender myself to Him and make bold to deal with Him, believing without doubt that He will be to me and do to me just what is said of Him.[1]

Luther then points out that what is affirmed in the creeds is that we believe *in* God, not that we believe God or *about* God.

This has been called an existentialist way of knowing. The emphasis is not upon the *being* of God or of human being, as abstract entity, but on *existence:* the living, sensing quality. Twentieth-century philosopher Michael Polanyi delineated this in an influential book, *Personal Knowing*. It is his assertion that personal knowing is the deepest and most real form of knowing.

Kierkegaard, referred to earlier, usually preferred the personal form of theologizing in his writings. He did not think that the God who is revealed in the Bible can be written about other than in personal terms. He opens a brief devotional book entitled *Purity of Heart* with these words:

Father in heaven! What is a man without Thee! What is all that he knows, vast accumulation though it be, but a chipped fragment if he does not know Thee! What is all his striving, could it even encompass a world, but a half-finished work if he does not know Thee: Thee the One, who art one thing and who art all! So may Thou give to the intellect, wisdom to comprehend that one thing; to the heart, sincerity to receive this understanding; to the will, purity that wills only one thing.[2]

The Bible speaks subjectively, or in personal terms, about God. The Bible is basically the story of God's relationship with people. Individuals receive words from God, speak to God, and respond either by obeying or rejecting what God commands, desires, or offers. The words of the prophets are not philosophical reflections. They are the words of the Lord to the people of Israel or Judah. Isaiah writes:

> And the Lord said:
> "Because this people draw near with their mouth
> and honor me with their lips
> while their hearts are far from me,
> and their fear of me is a commandment of men learned by
> rote;
> therefore, behold, I will again do marvelous things with this
> people,
> wonderful and marvelous; and the wisdom of their wise men
> shall perish."
>
> (Isa. 29:13–14)

This passage speaks clearly about the nature of God. It says that God's wisdom and knowledge is such that God sees through all the pretenses of worship and service. God has an inner knowledge of people, while they choose to believe that they can give an outward appearance of devotion. Only people who are aware of this inner dimension of faith can cultivate the spiritual life. The relationship to God is deepened by the acceptance of the full knowledge that God has of each person. When Jesus said that there is nothing hidden that shall not be revealed, he may have been talking about eschatological events, but he might also have been including the personal knowledge that cannot be hidden from God.

There is a cognitive, rational way of knowing. Human beings are given minds with which to think, and to use the mind fully can be an uplifting experience—inspiring, in fact. There is a scientific method, and there are forms of learning that demand intellectual exactitude. Knowledge about the spiritual realm requires what Paul called "testing the spirits." Paul is saying that you will know true spirituality by the fruit. In Galatians he contrasts life in the flesh with life in the Spirit. The latter, he says, gives true freedom. The fruit of the Spirit is love, joy, peace, patience, kindness, goodness, faithfulness, gentleness, self-control (Gal. 5:22). Notice that these are qualities that can be shown only through association with other people. Life in the Spirit is not a solitary life.

Rational knowledge about God is a way of testing the devotional practices and feelings of the spiritual life. As Martin Buber points out (Chapter 4), the I-it relationship and the I-Thou relationship are two dimensions of complete knowledge. Objective knowledge and impersonal relationships dissuade people from obligation to one another. Subjective knowledge and personal relationship alone can lead to sentimentality.

Objectivity is essential if persons are to avoid trying to impose their assertions of truth about God on other people. Objectivity, as a way of understanding, helps people acknowledge the individual bias, realize its value, but keep it in perspective. Objectivity makes it possible to learn from the insights of other people, including those whose religious experience may come from another culture, or a religion different from one's own. The objective dimension links the seeker after God with all others who seek Truth. To the scientist, following an hypothesis through the rigid canons of research, there may be a dedication and singleness of purpose close to that of the religious devotee. A moment of insight brings the joy of discovery, a sense of unity and wholeness that may be similar to the vision of the mystic. Spiritual boundaries are wide.

Subjectivity

If that is objectivity, what then is subjectivity? This begins with the personal dimension as a valid way of knowing. It is an affirmation of the self as an important source of knowledge. Subjectivity rounds out the reality of knowledge by including this personal dimension. In this way, it also tests objectivity. If the so-called objective view runs counter to human experience, such knowledge is in need of more thought and research.

But the subjective view can also be a way of avoiding reality. Feelings can become a substitute for thinking. Experience swayed by feelings can cause a person to draw conclusions that experience influenced by rational thought would interpret differently. Some people live in a private world. They have a self-image that may be far from the impression others have of them. They view other people from this personal perspective. Some persons can do no wrong, according to this perspective. Other persons known by the same individual will never be trusted. Consider what this kind of distorted perspective could do to the spiritual life. The ability to discern God's purposes for the self or others would be deeply clouded.

Then there is the idealist who views reality through the lens of a particular vision of the world. To this person, spirituality is an ecstatic emotion generated by a dream of a perfect society, a vision of some Holy City restored on earth. Some people have formed communities dedicated to fulfilling such an ideal. New Harmony, Indiana, was settled by people led from England by Robert Owen, who believed that by devoted efforts they could create, as the town's name suggests, the microcosm of a perfect community. The Oneida Community in New York State also held such a hope in its early days. The spirituality binding the members of such utopian groups was their dedication to the constructing of a perfect human society. They did not reckon with the reality that nothing human can be perfect. Such an insight can come only out of a religious awareness that places human beings in the context of God's existence, and human creativity within the provenance of the work of the Creator God.

Some people strive to perfect their own lives. They believe that with right discipline they can root from themselves all the negative aspects that mar personal relationships, such as anger, selfishness, or pride. Their approach is different from that of the Buddhist, who strives to eliminate all desires. Perfectionists wish to refine desires: anger will be reformed into calm, selfishness will be transformed into concern for others, pride will be transmuted into humility.

Unhappily, the effort to achieve perfection makes a person more self-centered because of the need for continual monitoring toward self-improvement. Such people become angry with themselves and will frequently project this anger onto other people. They are so involved in striving for perfection that they lose any capacity for simply being open for the Holy Spirit to work in and through them toward their fulfillment as human beings.

Sometimes a person like this is continually trying to make other people perfect. A perfectionist may find it virtually impossible to work with other people, participate in a spiritual life group, or be reasonably comfortable in a particular congregation. There is a dissatisfaction with all groups from which there is no escape. The classical collects for the church year voice implicit criticism of this all-too-human attitude. For example:

> Almighty God, the fountain of all wisdom, you know our necessities before we ask and our ignorance in asking: have compassion on our weakness, and mercifully give us those things which for our unworthiness we dare not, and for our blindness we cannot ask; through the worthiness of your Son Jesus Christ our Lord, who lives and reigns with you and the Holy Spirit, one God, now and for ever. Amen.[3]

Another person who avoids reality is the one who dreams about living the spiritual life. Reading the works of people like

Teresa, John Donne, or Rufus Jones can give a beautiful feeling of uplift. The reader *feels* spiritual, but the feeling might be only an evanescent one. Growth in the spiritual life does not come easily, and semblance is not reality. The fearful possibility is that one can read about spirituality as a way of avoiding living spiritually. "Make me pure, Lord," prayed Augustine, and added, "but not yet." That is an all-too-human response in the development of the spiritual life. It is natural to be fearful of any process that might be life-changing. The Bible makes it clear that one may be open to the working of the Spirit, but no one can command or predict what the result will be. This possibility is too scary for some people. They are content with the vicarious experience to be obtained through reading.

Retreat into Privatism

The person who lapses into subjectivity as a way of avoiding the realities of the spiritual life is retreating into privatism. This can be a comfortable way of avoiding conflict. It was pointed out in the first chapter that the quest for security can be one reason for cultivating the spiritual life—although one that fails to embrace the nature of life with God.

Living in a privatized world is an effort to avoid the conflict that is inevitably present in relationships with other people. Sometimes avoidance is a necessity, for a person can be pushed too far by events and be in danger of a breakdown. Even the maximum amount of human resources is not always sufficient for a crisis situation. Withdrawal can be a healthy response. For others, the problem is not in the situation, but in the shallowness of the spiritual resources available within a particular person to deal with the crisis.

A solitary spirituality can be a way of avoiding even the thought of a painful or evil situation. Avoidance and withdrawal are not the same kind of response. The Buddhist monk may withdraw from the world and cultivate freedom from desire, but that same person may go into the community each day, seeking food. The monk shares a sense of the uncertainty of life while disciplining himself to rise beyond it. So it is with the Christian monastic who spends her or his life in prayer, but who also strives through constant intercession to mitigate the tragedy of human life and to bring human lives into some correspondence with the purposes of God.

The person who avoids conflict substitutes for reality imagined scenarios where everything is good, every person is improving, and the path of life is always onward and upward.

Some years ago, two scholars studied best-selling inspirational books in America under the title *Popular Religion*.[4] Some of the books originally surveyed are out-of-print, but it is an indication of the persistence of privatized religion that some are still being reprinted and read. The authors found several criteria underlying the content of inspirational books. These books assume the validity of the Judeo-Christian tradition. They inspire readers with the hope of salvation on some terms. They offer "techniques" for achieving serenity, salvation, or the good life. They are addressed to "everyday problems of everyday people." The writers characterize such books as "everyman's psychiatry" because they are read in an effort to solve problems by persons who either cannot afford psychiatry or for various reasons will not seek counseling.

Religion can become a means for easing the pain of decision making. Some people believe that this is promised if their wills are completely surrendered to God. They believe that subsequent decisions, being inspired by God, will be in their best interest whatever the outcome. God seems comfortably near and is never perceived as judgmental toward those who enjoy this closeness. Personal salvation is their goal. Society will improve when people become converted. The practice of religious faith is expected to bring happiness—sometimes through prestige, "success," and money. This suggestion is clear to viewers of Robert Schuller's televised Sunday service from the Crystal Cathedral at Garden Grove. They see introduced each week some handsome, successful person who has overcome obstacles and gives all the credit to God. Millions who watch tend to identify with that person. The implicit corollary is that if they are not enjoying success, it is because their faith has not been strong enough.

Health is another indirect benefit of spiritual living in the popular view. Spiritual healing is the hope of many people. Some believe that illness has been sent by God either for punishment or testing. Others believe that while God permits illness to occur, other factors are responsible, either in the person's own life, or from some outside evil source, such as Satan. To those who believe that healing comes only from faith, spiritual healing means that physical wholeness will be restored: disease will be healed and disability repaired. Sometimes this does happen. Sometimes this does not happen. Instead of experiencing healing, some people learn to live with a disability. Some develop a deeper understanding of other humans who are suffering. This awareness can bring a new dimension to the experience of a sufferer. Acceptance of the fact that some diseases may be incurable makes possible the personal acceptance of dying. Living in a private religious world with the belief that either stronger faith or the conquest of the wiles of Satan would restore a person to health might be only a way of hoping for unending life—here on earth. It does not express authentic spirituality.

The retreat into privatism also takes the form of seeking a special psychological state in order to enhance feelings and heighten awareness. Through such practices a person withdraws more into the self, although the purpose of effort is to improve the self. Psychiatrist Gerald G. May speaks of these efforts:

> . . . They need to be seen as ways of encouraging oneself to be more freely and deeply and directly responsive to God, rather than ways of engineering one's own salvation.
>
> This is sometimes a very difficult distinction to make. Once we find the capacity to alter our state of awareness, it is almost impossi-

ble to avoid being caught up on the hope of being able to commandeer ourselves towards God—or towards some other destination. The fact that we are learning more effective ways of influencing our brains, bodies, and biochemistries means that we can be more willing, healthful, and responsive recipients of God's call to us. It does not mean that we are better able to play God.[5]

People who are cultivating religious paths to spiritual growth need to be aware of these temptations.

Monasticism at its best gives a different example. Monastic communities are made up of people who have voluntarily made a commitment to leave their geographical and family communities in order to build a life within an intentional community. Even in Eastern Orthodox monasteries where solitude takes up much of the day, there are times for worship together. Hermits unwittingly attract visitors by their solitary lifestyle, which seems to endow them with an aura of holiness. Members of a monastic community can no more withdraw from human relationships than can persons in a natural family. Likewise, the participants in any form of community life have to face the tensions that come from living together.

But their purposefulness incorporates two goals to which each person who seeks entrance becomes committed. One is a sustained and deliberate cultivation of the spiritual life through meditation, contemplation, prayer, liturgy, reading of the Bible and other writings, and through the acceptance of a designated person as spiritual director to assist in the process. The second goal is to express their spirituality, their relationship to God in love and adoration, by means of works through which to convey the love of God to people in the wider community. This work varies with the intention of each religious order and may be accomplished through preaching, teaching, evangelization, the founding of hospitals, or working among the poor and oppressed. Mindful of the parable of the Last Judgment, which points out those who truly recognize the Lord, they have established orphanages, carried on a ministry to prisoners, fed the hungry, and assisted the dying. The flexibility of each goal is illustrated by the ways in which ancient forms of service have been renewed in each century.

Viewing the development of the spiritual life as a retreat into privacy is also found wanting when seen in the perspective of the Bible. The roots of social justice invariably come from prophets who remained quiet long enough to hear the word of the Lord but who then went among people to proclaim it. Elijah, fresh from the victory of Carmel and recognizing that success meant danger for him, fled to Horeb, the holy mountain. As he was fasting there, God became present to him not in wind, earthquake, and fire—the traditional ways—but in a still, small voice that told him to anoint a new king for Syria, a new king for Israel, and a successor to himself. God's judgment was proclaimed in action, and the continuance of the prophetic calling was assured.

Jesus left the wilderness into which he had gone after his baptism, and immediately began preaching the good news (Mark 1:14). He took the disciples apart to mourn the death of John only to find that the crowd had followed them and needed to be fed (Mark 6:30f). He went from prayer in the Garden of Gethsemane to the judgment halls of Caiaphas and Pilate and thence to the Cross.

During the fifteenth century, a new impetus toward world mission took its start from that remarkable company called the Society of Jesus. Their founder, Ignatius Loyola, himself a former soldier who had been wounded in battle, likened the order to an army, disciplined for every task. They were committed to rigorous periods of study and prayer and given a routine to assist in their spiritual development. Some traveled as far away as China, immersing themselves in that great culture, the better to understand how the Chinese might come to understand the gospel.

Three young men, students at Williams College in New England early in the nineteenth century, gathered under a haystack during a thunderstorm. There they vowed to devote their lives to God. One of them, Adoniram Judson, made the long voyage to Burma, where he spent the rest of his life learning the language and absorbing the culture in order to communicate the love of God in Christ. Innumerable others have followed similar routes, hearing a call to assist the poor, feed the hungry, heal the sick, and teach people to know the love of God as they were themselves experiencing this love. Private spirituality could never have accomplished these kinds of goals.

Today, a missionary outreach is to be found in other religions. The East has come to the West. Forms of Hinduism and Buddhism, brought by devoted exemplars, have answered needs felt by former Christians and Jews who have either rejected or not understood their own traditions of spirituality. Many such Westerners have learned from Eastern religions to look inward in order to cultivate the spiritual life. They have accepted personal goals for holiness, sometimes within a separate community as among the Rama Krishnas, and sometimes as converts without withdrawing from their accustomed ways of life.

Others seek a private spirituality within a Christian framework. They do not see the irony in the gospel story when Jesus' invitation to the disciples—"Come ye apart"—ended with a command to feed the multitude.

Another form of privatism may be for personal adjustment. For some people, withdrawal is not done primarily for the purpose of re-entering the arena with new strength. Solitude may be chosen in order to view the self in relation to a life situation, and see where it is possible to adjust in order to meet opposition more amicably, diffuse conflict, and avoid power struggles. Adjusting to a situation can be a realistic mode of self-preservation. Feeling defeated is rarely a gain. But "adjustment" as a goal can also make it possible for a person to evade difficult decisions and actions.

Retreat in Order to Gain Strength

Spirituality through retreat may become the best way to renew strength. By withdrawing from an immediate situation a
person may be able to see it in perspective. A breathing space
is gained; the pattern of life becomes clear. One may have
been bound by the expectations of other people, as well as the
expectations of the self. There may have been an assumption
that the path is set and nothing can change—either for better
or for worse. Life becomes a treadmill and each task monotonous. As in the folk-saying about not being able to see the
forest for the trees, a person can feel lost in such a situation.
One is neither meeting conflict nor avoiding it, but merely
becoming so caught up in it as to be unable to see either issues
or solutions.

Have you ever been on the top of a hill, overlooking a city?
I have. All visitors to Toledo, Spain, should see that view of the
city from the hills across the river (at the present *parador*),
which the artist El Greco saw as he sketched there. The whole
plan of the city becomes evident: the location of the cathedral
and its relation to the Alcazar; the way in which houses and
streets seem to wind down toward the river; the extent of the
wall; the way in which the river seems to encircle the city like
a moat, forming a natural boundary. Before viewing the city
from this vantage point a visitor wandered up and down the
narrow streets, unable to find the cathedral for all its size because of the encroaching buildings. But here it stands out
clearly as Toledo's crowning jewel.

Perhaps you have been traveling along an interstate highway
with some crests and turns. At one moment, you are at the top
of a hill, and the double ribbon of road lies in front of you for
miles. You still cannot see your destination (although sometimes a city will appear in the distance), but you have a feeling
for the entire route.

This is the kind of perspective every person needs. It cannot
be found while one is immersed in places or events; nor is it

disclosed in the clamor of many voices. The purpose of retreat at this point is to clarify purposes, goals, and the course of action. Wisdom comes through meditating on life in the presence of God; reviewing a situation in calm assurance. Anxiety is replaced by confidence, confusion by clarity, weakness by strength. Renewed in mind and spirit, one becomes like a new person. Wholeness returns to a divided self. The voices become unified.

The prophet writes:

They who wait for the Lord shall renew their strength,
They shall mount up with wings like eagles,
They shall run and not be weary, they shall walk and not faint.
(Isa. 40:31)

This can be the experience of those who retreat in order to gain strength.

A new perspective brings a larger vision. The undergrowth has been cut away, as in some carefully tended forest preserve cultivated for the delight of its owner. Clarity leads to vision (both words pertain to sight). Those who are spiritually aware are enabled to see the capabilities of each person and the possibilities in each situation. It is not coincidental that spiritual seers frequently recount their visions when they have seen Christ present or heard the Divine Voice. This could happen because they were attentive. They expected the Vision, although they did not know in advance when it would come. They listened for the Voice, although they had no foreknowledge of the Presence. Vision does not simply inform a person how to improve the task. Vision may lead in a totally new direction, toward a hitherto unthought-of goal. "Beyond our wildest dreams" is a colloquial phrase that describes the actual situation that may develop for those who patiently and sincerely seek spiritual renewal.

In the spiritual quest one is not left to carry out the Vision alone. God grants power for its fulfillment. The Holy Spirit is dynamic, in the sense of the biblical *dunamis,* a Greek word meaning "power," from which comes the word "dynamic." The realization of power is one of the signs of growth in the spiritual life. This is different from the all-too-human use of power to overcome the weak, enforce one's will, and enhance status. Biblical images for the power of God are many, but that power is given only to those who are receptive and is never forced upon anyone. This power is shown in gentleness, kindness, and long-suffering. The power exhibited through Jesus would scarcely commend itself to the powers that rule over national destinies. That is the whole point of the famous dialogue between Jesus and the Grand Inquisitor, representing the temporal power of the church, in Dostoyevski's novel *The Brothers Karamazov*. You will recall that the Grand Inquisitor suggested that Jesus would have to be destroyed in order that the church in its power might survive.

Spiritual power does not come easily. Earlier, reference was made to the "dark night of the soul," a phrase made memorable by John of the Cross. In popular terms, this has been interpreted to mean those times of "dryness" in the spiritual life, during which God seems to be absent. This happens partly because we mistakenly construe a "happening" to be an activity. Waiting, in our minds, is not activity: nothing "happens." But to those deeply imbued with the life of the Spirit, dry times are part of their spiritual growth. The very fact that a person is aware that the sense of Presence has gone indicates that there has been such an experience, and hints at a return. This "dark night" does not imply being overwhelmed by life, work, or circumstances, but of being enveloped by the Divine Presence, yet being unable, because of darkness, to be able to discern this Presence. How ironic it seems to the believer! One withdraws in order to see with more clarity, but for awhile one cannot see at all.

The eventual reward of those who retreat, not in order to avoid life, but in order to meet life, is renewed strength, and the power that can come from God alone.

Teaching for a Balanced Spirituality

The point being made here is that some people seek growth in the spiritual life in order to avoid the conflicts of life. Actually they seek a way of withdrawal. Others seek growth in the spiritual life in order to meet conflict. How can the educative process contribute to a withdrawal that is strengthening rather than weakening, that equips people for struggle rather than protecting them from struggle?

To begin with, it is important for people to become aware that there are both objective and subjective elements in the spiritual life. There is an inwardness through which a person can come to know the self better. It is not an easy process, because there are some forms of knowledge a person would rather avoid. To say "Who am I?" is to see oneself in relation to God.

The Bible is a primary source for this kind of subjective knowledge. People in the Bible are so human that we would sometimes rather not identify with them. We would rather be like John, leaving the nets in order to response to the call of Jesus, than like John, who responded in anger to the people who would not let the disciples enter their village. We would rather be like Peter making his confession of faith than Peter denying the Lord. Subjective knowledge in the best sense probes all dimensions of personality. We teach this by giving people opportunities to identify with biblical people in *all* their experiences, exploring how their lives are like ours, and how the transforming power that was in them can be in us. These stories can be used for small-group study and individual meditation. The stories can be narrated and group members be asked to study events, identify with persons, meditate on the meaning, and seek for themselves the source of strength.

Another subjective source of self-knowledge may be found in hymns and other religious poetry. Literary forms do not so much try to tell readers *about* people or situations, as to help the reader identify with and participate in that life. Consider this hymn from seventeenth-century Spain:

> My God, I love thee; not because / I hope for heaven thereby,
> Nor yet for fear that loving not, / I might forever die;
> Not with the hope of gaining aught, / not seeking a reward;
> But as thyself hast loved me, / O ever-loving Lord!

Poet Francis Thompson expresses the ambiguity in the relationship to God in the poem "The Hound of Heaven":

> I fled Him, down the nights and down the days;
> I fled Him down the arches of the years;
> I fled Him, down the labyrinthine ways
> Of my own mind; and in the mist of tears
> I hid from Him, and under running laughter.

People are helped to deepen the spiritual life when they realize that God is known most clearly through his relationship to mankind. The Bible records this in many ways. God is the awesome one: near yet distant. YHWH is the unpronounceable name denoting the one who *is*. God is known in burning bush, in fire and cloud from the mountain, but also in words of yearning tenderness toward a people gone astray. To see this side of God in the biblical narrative is to become aware that "knowing" God is on a different plane from knowing about God. The methods for conveying this kind of knowledge are specific: narrative, drama, hymn, poetry, and personal message.

In Jeremiah we read:

> For thus says the Lord:
> Your hurt is incurable,
>   and your wound is grievous.
> There is none to uphold your cause,
>   no medicine for your wound,
>   no healing for you.
> All your lovers have forgotten you;
>   they care nothing for you; . . .
> Why do you cry out over your hurt?
>   Your pain is incurable.

> Because your guilt is great,
>   because your sins are flagrant,
>   I have done these things to you. . . .
> For I will restore health to you,
>   and your wounds I will heal, says the Lord.
>
> (Jer. 30:12-14)

The experience of others in the spiritual life is also helpful to us. Those known through their writing centuries ago can still be known today. The journey is shared by means of such mutual strengthening along the way.

Meditation on the creeds assists toward becoming aware of the personal nature of knowing. At one's baptism, the Apostles' Creed is repeated, according to liturgical tradition. In recent liturgical renewal it is becoming customary at a baptismal service for those already baptized to renew their vows by affirming the Creed along with the candidates for baptism and, in the case of infants, their sponsors. To meditate on the statement "I believe *in* God . . . *in* Jesus . . . *in* the Holy Spirit" is a way of reminding all concerned to be always aware of the personal knowledge involved in commitment.

The Nicene Creed brings another dimension to this personal knowledge, because it was written in the first person plural, the "we" form. This statement of faith is the affirmation of a believing people. Issued by a council of bishops in the year 325, and always controversial because of the way in which it attempts to state both the divine and human character of Jesus Christ, it is distinctive in that it affirms a corporate faith, in distinction from the assertion of an individual faith found in the Apostles' Creed. This too is a "believing *in*" statement.

The other side of the coin is the necessity for a rational faith. These two affirmations of faith need to be studied in many dimensions. To examine what is meant by the terms "God," "Father," "Almighty," "Creator," is the work of theology, an intellectual discipline. Some might find it surprising that intellectual inquiry should be considered an element in spiritual development. Yet without reason, as has been noted earlier, faith diminishes into sentimentality. The powerful assertion that God became a human being, lived among us, poured out his life for us, and rose from the dead to assure us that we share eternal life is central to Christian faith. But the picture of Jesus of Nazareth that comes through in some hymns and poetry suggests all sweetness and light. In another view Jesus seems almost an abstraction; simply a vessel through whom the divine reconciliation could be accomplished. There is a powerful difference between saying that he "bought" our salvation and that he "wrought" our salvation.

Just as philosophical knowledge about God and the elements of faith are essential to full understanding, so objective knowledge about human beings helps to round out the picture of why people seek spiritual foundations as they do. Rational knowledge "tests" subjective knowledge. Each is essential. We can sentimentalize about ourselves and about other people. It is easy to see ourselves as better than we are. That bolsters the ego. Some tend to denigrate the self, emphasizing their sinfulness, seeming to live without hope of redemption. A balanced spirituality that views personal bias realistically can be taught. Self-examination is an ancient spiritual discipline. Carried too far it can become narcissistic and damaging. Exaggerations in either direction, whether toward personal goodness or evil are detrimental to growth. But meditating on both weaknesses and strengths in the presence of God makes self-examination an essential element in spiritual growth.

Another important element in the educational process is to help persons learn to balance the personal need for spiritual fulfillment with the expression of the spiritual life in a community. There has been a tendency toward quietism among Christians. This is a belief that one can so withdraw the will in passivity, that one becomes completely subject to the will of God. The Quietist attitudes of the Port Royalists in seventeenth-century France brought papal rebuke after they expressed the view that there was no need to view their mode of living in relation to the beliefs and practices of the whole church. Pietis-

tic Protestantism sometimes approximates this view. Modern
Protestants who value personal prayer more than congregational worship ignore the fact that the world "liturgy" means
"common work": the Sunday worship service expresses individual devotion and at the same time strengthens it.

Many people believe that they can cultivate the spiritual life
alone. They do not understand that interaction with others results in a deepened spirituality. They avoid the distractions of
having other people around as well as what they view as the
distraction of hearing hymns or sermons that might be disturbing. They become unable to pray *through* the liturgy.

The monastic life wisely includes both corporate and individual prayer. In the formation of Roman Catholic theological
seminaries, this interaction has always been understood, although the forms by which it is expressed may change. Teaching for a balanced spirituality requires equal emphasis on attendance at and reflection upon the corporate work of
worship, and an increased proficiency in personal forms of
prayer.

An extension of the need for a relationship to a worshipping
community is the need for a relationship to wider neighborhood, national, and world communities. Issues that affect and
afflict people in every part of the globe will not be evaded by a
deeply spiritual person. Teaching for a balanced spirituality
will include opportunities for people to learn about these needs,
ways of using intercession (both alone and in the company of
others) to lift these needs into the presence of God, and opportunities for actual service to others.

There is a story about a monk living during the Middle Ages
whose particular responsibility was to open the door of the
monastery at noon each day in order to distribute a daily ration
to the poor. One day, during an intense moment of prayer and
adoration, Christ appeared to the monk in his cell. At that moment the noonday bell sounded. The monk heard the bell. He
also saw the Figure. He hesitated. To leave his cell would be
rude, irreverent, even sacrilegious. On the other hand, he was

committed to absolute obedience, and to serve the poor at this hour was his assigned task

The monk, answering the summons, left his cell, opened the door, and distributed the bread.

When he returned, the Lord was still there. "I was afraid," whispered the monk, again returning to awed contemplation. "I was afraid that if I left, you would not be here when I returned."

"Did you think I would leave my poor ones?" came the reply. "Had you not gone to feed them, then I would have left in order to do so."

Finally, teaching a balanced spirituality can help people develop new perspective and fresh vision by offering them opportunities to get away from their immediate situations. The spiritual retreat is designed to do this. Unfortunately, "retreat," in some Protestant usage, is frequently only a synonym for conference, for which a program is carefully planned, speakers are selected, discussions arranged, and worship services structured. There is little opportunity for silence, introspection, listening to the Bible, or waiting on God. Many people today are uneasy with silence. They need to be trained to enjoy it, and taught how to use it to strengthen their spiritual lives. A careful balance between speaking and listening, presentation and reflection, corporate worship and personal prayer is difficult to discover in many forms of so-called retreat.

On the other hand, the classical pattern of the silent retreat may be a form appreciated only by those who are well along in the development of the spiritual life. Those who have participated in such a retreat often note that it is easier to have the sugar or cream passed during a breakfast eaten in silence, when each person tends to be alert to the needs of the neighbor, than it is at a conference where everyone is so busy talking that no one is aware of what anyone else needs. This may be exaggerated, but it points to the sensitivity to others engendered by silence. It suggests also the possible cultivation of sensitivity to one's own needs, and potential openness to the work of the Holy Spirit.

Retreatants are refreshed and strengthened by the subject matter of the retreat, which can give them new perspectives on their responsibilities to others, add new dimensions to the Christian way of life, and offer new opportunities to look inward to their own needs, new refreshment from personal prayer and shared worship, and new strength from a relaxed and unhurried atmosphere in a place set apart. They can return to everyday life with less need to avoid the conflicts of life because they have found new strength to meet life on any level.

6. Roots of Spirituality

A mature understanding of spirituality comes when there is an appreciation for its roots. Lasting spiritual nurture and development are made stronger when built on this foundation.

Theological Roots

The theological roots of spirituality come from God-consciousness deep within a person. To say that everyone has this consciousness would be an unprovable assertion, but an awareness of the Transcendent does seem to be universal. There are evidences that human beings, long before a time of recorded history, maintained rituals that pointed to divine intervention into their lives, especially at birth and death.

This consciousness is an awareness of the existence of Someone or Something, a Power beyond the self and greater than any human being. Even the philosophers in the eighteenth-century Age of Enlightenment, who would not accept the idea of a personal God, affirmed that there was a power that created the universe and keeps it in motion. The hymn "The Spacious Firmament on High," echoing this thought, comes from Haydn's oratorio *The Creation*, which reflects exalted wonder at the orderliness of the created universe. A sense of the impersonal Transcendent was the source of spirituality for people of broad intellectual interests and creative abilities such as Benjamin Franklin and Thomas Jefferson.

A similar sense of wonder informs the spirituality of those who find God in the natural world. The seemingly infinite blanket of stars across the night sky and the cloudless blue stretching to the horizon across flat plains are complemented by the majesty of snow-capped mountains or meadows blanketed with colorful wildflowers. The work of a Divine Creator is revealed to some observers in the orderly composition of a flower, the well-articulated flight of a bird, or the frail loveliness of a butterfly. The roar of the ocean, the flow of a river, the stillness of a woodland pool, all evoke a feeling of the spiritual. A person thinks, "I could not make this," then adds, "I do not believe that it could have developed without a purposeful Creator."

This rationale for a Transcendent Spirit works as long as the natural world can be seen as beneficent. What happens to such spirituality when the ocean is whipped by winds into a typhoon or hurricane, or when the rivers, fed by mountain snows, rush wildly on their course, carrying away houses, destroying crops, and causing the deaths of people? Even the life-giving sun can beat down mercilessly (mercy being a human and divine quality) without cloud or rain, causing crops to wither, and people to succumb to famine.

If one believes in a deity who created the world and ordered it in such a way as to exist on its own momentum, such problems do not arise. God is not responsible for the extremes of nature. Human beings have a responsibility to prepare for natural disasters. They do not have to live on a flood plain. But when people find their source of adoration in a power that created the beauty and mystery of the natural world, they will eventually have to face the fact that any part of creation can be either beneficent or demonic. The existence of evil raises questions about the nature of the Transcendent. Pain, suffering, and death are inescapable on this earth, whether the responsibility rests with God, an evil power (Satan), or human beings.[1]

In spite of such problems, spirituality is based on the affirmation that there is One greater than human beings, not limited by the frailties of humanity, and in touch with a universe so vast that we have only begun to explore it.

Another source of the consciousness of God lies in a sense of a near Presence. This is referred to as the "immanence" of

God. It is at another pole from transcendence because it evokes a feeling of closeness. The question of how God is present in the world is one that has challenged the thought of theologians ever since people have tried to understand the nature and activity of God. If it is affirmed that God is in the world in a literal sense, then every tree or flower, every bird or human being is, to some extent, God. The Creator and the created become merged. This belief has a technical name: pantheism, meaning that God is in all things. This is not an option for people of the Bible because in the scriptures God is made known as One who is separate from the world. God's will is known through the events of history. God is self-revealed to kings and prophets through words, dreams, and actions. As was indicated in Chapter 2, the Spirit of God is the Revealer of God.

Revelation could not take place if God were in a person because the knowledge of God would already be present. The biblical idea of revelation presupposes that God is transcendent; that is, he has and is a personal being, and deliberately descends (in Paul's words even "condescends") to enter into human existence. In the biblical understanding, God is the initiator. That is the meaning of revelation: literally to remove the veils, to make clear that which was hidden.

A particular kind of spirituality derives from this view of the immanence of God. Only a person can deeply be in touch with other persons. Only when there is a separateness of persons can there be a reaching toward the other, for this must be a voluntary action. Individuality makes possible the reciprocity of seeking and responding. Prayer requires this responsiveness. The relationship of which Martin Buber writes in *I and Thou* could derive only from a biblical understanding of God. Revelation is the self-disclosure of God, and through this knowledge of God, people come into a deeper understanding of themselves. They see themselves in the perspective of the holiness of the Transcendent One who seeks to enter into the life of the human world.

The contrast between the divine and human becomes a creative factor in the growth of the spiritual life. A new perspective on life is granted, and new opportunities for sharing in the Divine Life are perceived. This process differs from that of reflection or meditation, which can take place as a human activity. In that kind of reflection people concentrate on themselves, aspiring to overcome the evil in them in order to become more perfectly what a human being should be. Revelation indicates to the believer what Søren Kierkegaard once called the infinite qualitative distance between God and human beings. The sense of wonder arises from the perception of the kind of love that would cause God to become involved in the tangled history human beings have developed. This involvement evokes awe, similar to that experienced by the person who finds God revealed in the natural world. In addition, personal revelation— the knowledge of God that comes through human encounter— brings an awareness of sin. The knowledge that sin and evil are part of human experience helps a person to cope with this so that the spiritual life is not destroyed. The acceptance of reality gives a dimension to the spiritual life. Revelation, in the biblical sense, assumes the healing presence in the world of God, who makes all things new.

This leads to another aspect of God-consciousness: the relationship between the human quest and the divine initiative; the difference between seeking and being sought. Human beings value their autonomy. They like to feel that they initiate events; they endeavor to direct their own lives. They also like to believe that they seek God and that they find God. This understanding of God can be derived from contemplating the work of God in the natural world. It can also be found by thinking about God, reading what philosophers and theologians have said, discussing the subject with others, and then coming to some personally satisfying conclusions about the nature of God. Through such activity, a person certainly gains some understanding of who God is, what God is like, and what kind of relationship is possible.

Many people go through periods of life when they are look-ing for God. Young adults, who once accepted the beliefs nur-tured through home, church, and community, reach an age where they want to find answers for themselves. They are seeking God. Old adults may feel that life is not reflecting the God in whom they have believed. They feel abandoned by God. God is hidden from them and they cannot be certain that God exists. They too are seeking. They may not expect a revelation from God, but they hope for some sign of God's beneficent existence.

There is validity in Buber's insight that we cannot know a person fully through our own searching. Persons reveal what they will and hide what they will. If God is personal, then God will take the initiative. This affirmation is derived from the biblical way of understanding God. God is the initiator, but God can be depended upon to want to be known. God loves, cares, seeks, guides, offers help—all these active verbs de-scriptive of God occur in the Bible. God is not in hiding, wait-ing to be found. The relationship is one of mutuality and reci-procity.

Jeremiah writes to the people of Jerusalem exiled in Baby-lon: "You will call upon me and come and pray to me, and I will hear you: you will seek me, and find me; when you seek me with all your heart, I will be found by you, says the Lord" (Jer. 29:12–14a). Note the use of the passive verb. There is a subtle quality of word use here that leaves the initiative with God while acknowledging the necessity for human response. The spiritual life is deepened by continual openness to the ini-tiative of God's self-revelation.

The consciousness of God takes on a new dimension through the Christian understanding of God as Trinity. The term has often led to misunderstanding. It sounds as if Christians wor-ship three gods, particularly when they address prayer to Jesus, rather than in the name of Jesus. The Holy Spirit seems to be less a part of God and more a generalized presence separate from God. It might even seem that Christians had two gods, Jesus Christ being one of them. How then can a doctrine so complicated be an enrichment for the spiritual life?

As a description of the fullness of God, who God is and how God acts, the idea of God as Trinity can add dimension to spirituality. Stated as an intellectual assertion that attempts to define God, it would be presumptuous. As a reflection on how God is understood and experienced within the Christian community, it is a useful descriptive summary of One who is both transcendent and immanent. The summary is most succinctly made in the Apostles' Creed, which is the ancient Roman symbol and the traditional baptismal affirmation of faith. This describes God as the Creator, an understanding with which most theistically oriented religious people would concur. (The adjective "almighty" denotes power; the term "Father" suggests progenitor, but can also have a personal dimension). The next description is the specifically Christian affirmation that God was revealed in Jesus Christ: his humanity, his suffering, resurrection, and eternal life with God. This "humanizing" of God has been a powerful image for asserting that God has so completely shared in human life as to be forever "on our side" and intimately connected with humanity as a transcendent God could not be. God is further revealed by the continuing activity of the Holy Spirit through the church and the lives of committed individuals. This is the power of God through whom the divine purposes are fulfilled. The understanding of the Spirit contrasts with and completes the assertion that God acts through the created universe. It continues the long biblical witness to the activity of God in Israel, the covenant community, through patriarchs, prophets, and kings.

Meditation on the three aspects of God and the Oneness of God revealed as Trinity is a powerful dimension for the spiritual life. It is an assertion of the mystery of God and of the human inability to define God. How can one separate a person and at the same time unite the parts? Analogies are used in an attempt to explain God as Trinity: the actor wearing three masks, the several roles that each person plays in the relationships of life, the kinds of activity in which people become involved. Human analogies are imperfect. If the understanding of God as Trinity leads to an awareness of the transcendent mystery of God and the limitations of human attempts at understanding God beyond God's own revelation, then it can be a useful concept in spiritual development.

Biblical Roots

The first chapter of Genesis sets the tone: it proclaims the wonder of God's activity in words that evoke awe in the hearer. No one can read this passage without perceiving a crescendo of power. Each section begins with "And God said, 'Let there be,'" and ends with "And God saw that it was good." The work of creation is completed with the blessing of the Sabbath. Later, the covenant of the rainbow is a sign both of the power and the concern of the Creator. The relationship of Abraham to God is a reminder of divine revelation and human response.

The presence of the transcendent God filled the community from the time that the Hebrews encamped in the Sinai and developed a sense of becoming a covenant people. After the dramatic events of the giving of the Law, the worship of the golden calf, and the assembling of the tabernacle, we read:

> Whenever Moses went out to the tent, all the people rose up, and every man stood at his tent door, and looked after Moses, until he had gone into the tent. When Moses entered the tent, the pillar of cloud would descend and stand at the door of the tent, and the Lord would speak with Moses.
>
> And when all the people saw the pillar of cloud standing at the door of the tent, all the people would rise up and worship, every man at his tent door. (Exod. 33:8-10)

Centuries later, the tent was gone, and the Ark of the covenant was now secluded within the holy of holies of the Temple built by King Solomon. At the dedication he prayed:

> But will God dwell indeed with man on the earth? Behold, heaven
> and the highest heaven cannot contain thee; how much less this
> house which I have built! Yet have regard to the prayer of thy
> servant and to his supplication, O Lord my God, hearkening to the
> cry and to the prayer which they servant prays before thee; that thy
> eyes may be open day and night toward this house, the place where
> thou has promised to set thy name. . . . (2 Chron. 6:18-20)

The early Christian community developed a sense of awe in
the presence of the risen Lord. Matthew ends his gospel with a
gathering of the disciples in Galilee, saying, "When they saw
him, they worshipped him; but some doubted" (Matt. 28:11).
There was ambiguity in the recognition of who he might be.
Jesus assures them, "Lo, I am with you always, to the close of
the age" (Matt. 20). The two disciples at Emmaus, after their
eyes were opened (note the passive voice: the revelation *to*
them) said: "Did not our hearts burn within us while he talked
to us on the road, while he opened to us the Scriptures?"
(Luke 24:32). Some of the Twelve were fishing on Lake Galilee when, following commands from a person on the shore,
they suddenly found their nets full. One cried out, "It is the
Lord!" (John 21:7). There is a note of awe and wonder in those
words. The Transcendent had drawn near in some mysterious
way. It was not their doing; the Presence was a gift.

No more vivid description of the power of God entering into
a human gathering can be found than in the account of Pentecost:

> And suddenly a sound came from heaven like the rush of a mighty
> wind, and it filled all the house where they were sitting. And there
> appeared to them tongues as of fire, distributed and resting on each
> one of them. And they were all filled with the Holy Spirit and
> began to speak in other tongues, as the Spirit gave them utterance.
> (Acts 2:2-4)

The onlookers, whom the account describes as "devout men
from every nation under heaven," were "amazed and per-
plexed, saying to one another, What does this mean?" (Acts
12). But the writer, with the candor of those who wrote scrip-

ture, adds, "But others mocking said, 'They are filled with new wine' " (13).

Nowhere is the human response to the transcendent glory of God more dramatically described than in The Revelation to John, with its heavenly liturgy:

> Holy, holy, holy is the Lord God Almighty, who was, and is, and is to come. (Rev. 4:8)
> To him who sits upon the throne, and to the Lamb be blessing and honor and glory and might for ever and ever! (Rev. 5:13)

The sense of the transcendence of God is one facet of the biblical roots of spirituality. Another is to be found in the stories of people who heard God's call and the ways in which they responded. Noah might have refused the call to build the boat. Everybody thought it was an absurd idea. But in the calm that followed the storm and flood, when Noah erected an altar and made an offering to the Lord, the promise came that "while the earth remains, seedtime and harvest, cold and heat, summer and winter, day and night shall not cease" (Gen. 8:22).

In a comment on people of faith, the writer of the Letter to the Hebrews says, "By faith Abraham obeyed when he was called to go out to a place which he was to receive as an inheritance; and he went out, not knowing where he was to go" (Heb. 11:8). Most of the family stayed at Haran.

The relevation to Moses in the burning bush should have been evidence to Moses of a revelation of God's presence. Moses, having investigated the bush out of curiosity, had to be told that this was holy ground. But even though he hid his face in awe, he was bold enough to protest his lack of qualifications for standing before Pharaoh to demand the release of his people. This was his hour of decision, and because he answered "yes" to God, the five books of Moses can end with the tribute, "There has not arisen a prophet since in Israel like Moses, whom the Lord knew face to face" (Deut. 34:10).

One could continue with the stories of people who evaded

the call, refused the call, or were faithless to the call—as well as those who were faithful.

Jesus answered the call: at his baptism, through the temptation, in the ministry, and by all the events of the Passion. The writer of the Letter to the Hebrews comments: "Tempted at all points as we are, yet without sin" (Heb. 4:15). In his Resurrection the glory of God is revealed.

Peter is the disciple whose experience parallels that of most people. He responded to the call, leaving his daily work, to entrust his life and that of his family to Jesus. He rose to a high point of witness at Caesarea Philippi as the company turned toward Jerusalem, when he affirmed to Jesus: "You are the Messiah." He wavered during the trial of Jesus, fearful for his own life, and denied that he had ever known the man. Like the others, he was absent when the Cross was lifted up. Still, he recovered faith enough to recognize the risen Lord and be forgiven. He risked imprisonment and death at Jerusalem for his witness to Christ and even, after some initial hesitancy, baptized Gentiles, Cornelius and his family, who had already been granted the gift of the Holy Spirit. But the "old" Simon reappeared later. When a council was called at Jerusalem to decide whether circumcision should be prerequisite to baptism, Peter agreed with the Jewish Christians and was roundly condemned by Paul, who insinuated that Peter spoke one opinion in Jerusalem but another when among the Gentiles. Tradition says that Peter later won the martyr's crown at Rome, dying by crucifixion. He was faithful to the call in the ambiguous way that most people are.

Finally, there is the apostle Paul, who resisted the call yet was granted an expression of the Lord's Presence so powerful as to have resulted in the surrender of the remainder of his life to Christ. Paul seemed almost to glory in danger and even to court controversy. No one was more active than he in the proclamation of the gospel. The roots of this life are apparent in the letters. He speaks of spiritual gifts (1 Cor. 12): "No one can say

'Jesus is Lord' except by the Holy Spirit. Now there are varieties of gifts, but the same Spirit" (3,4). "For by one Spirit we
were all baptized into one body" (13). He writes that the Spirit
prevented him from going to Bithynia. But the Spirit sent him
to other places. His life was constantly lived in the Spirit of
God. He affirmed that "in everything God works for good with
those who love him" (Rom. 8:28), and "I can do all things in
him who strengthens me" (Phil. 4:13). Paul epitomizes an active spirituality. Ceaselessly traveling around the cities of eastern Asia, he felt both compelled and empowered to proclaim
the good news that had changed his life.

The Psalms are primary literature for the spiritual life. Praying the Psalms has been the devotional path for believers for
three thousand years. These songs take a variety of forms.
Some are hymns of praise used in Temple worship. Some are
hymns sung by pilgrims on their way to Jerusalem. Others reveal the personal anguish and anxiety of the writers. Some are
bitter laments through which the writer vents frustration on
God. Because of his deeply human quality, the Psalms have
been models of prayer for Jews and Christians, in liturgy and
personal devotion.

Psalms reveal the nature of a God who cares, comforts, and
redeems. God so loves these human creatures as to be able to
receive the anger they express at the injustice of life. "Why
dost thou stand afar off, O Lord? Why dost thou hide thyself in
times of trouble?" the psalmist asks (Ps. 10:1).

No Psalm more powerfully voices the cry of the afflicted
than does Psalm 22, which Christians often have taken as a
meditation on the crucifixion. It begins, "My God, my God,
why hast thou forsaken me? . . . I cry by day but thou dost not
answer; and by night but find no rest." Remembrances of
God's past action bring reassurance: "Yet thou art holy, . . . in
thee our fathers trust; they trusted, and thou didst deliver
them" (Ps. 22:3,4). In a swing back to personal feelings there
follows the line made famous in the original of the hymn

"Amazing Grace." The writer says, "But I am a worm, and no man; scorned by men, and despised by the people" (6,7). This mood continues, until there is again a cry for help, "But thou, O Lord, be not far off! O thou my help, hasten to my aid!" (19). The Psalm ends with a joyful cry of deliverance: "From thee comes my praise in the great congregation; my vows I will pay before those who fear him" (25). The suppliant has been delivered and goes to the Temple to give thanks.

Other Psalms voice reassurance, such as Psalm 23, a song of quiet confidence. Or Psalm 46: "God is our refuge and strength, a very present help in trouble. Therefore we will not fear though the earth should change, and the mountains shake in the heart of the sea" (1,2). Psalm 84 begins:

> How lovely is thy dwelling place,
>   O Lord of hosts!
> My soul longs, yea, faints
>   for the courts of the LORD;
> my heart and flesh sing for joy
>   to the living God. (1,2)

Others are Psalms of praise and thanksgiving. Psalm 92 begins:

> It is good to give thanks to the Lord,
>   to sing praises to thy name, O Most High;
> to declare thy steadfast love in the morning,
>   and thy faithfulness by night. (1,2)

Psalm 96 includes the whole world in praise:

> O sing to the Lord a new song;
>   sing to the Lord, all the earth!
> Sing to the Lord, bless his name;
>   tell of his salvation from day to day.
> Declare his glory among the nations,
>   his marvelous works among all the peoples! (1-3)

Another type of Psalm is a meditation on the history of God's redemptive work for the people of Israel. Psalm 136 is an example. This Psalm praises God through the work of creation (a reflection on Genesis 1) and continues with the story of the flight from Egypt:

> O give thanks to the Lord, for he is good,
>   for his steadfast love endures for ever. . . .
> To him who alone does great wonders,
>   for his steadfast love endures for ever; . . .
> To him who divided the Red Sea in sunder,
>   for his steadfast love endures for ever. (1,4,13)

The Psalms have been integral to the liturgical life, first in the Jerusalem Temple for which some were written, now in synagogue and church. Monastic communities, with regular hours of community prayer, use the Psalms in a cycle once each month. Individuals cultivating the devotional life find in them a constant dialogue with God as they meditate on God and themselves in ways they might not otherwise have contemplated.

Psychological Roots: Self-consciousness

One root of spirituality is to be found in the self. It is only through self-awareness that one can be related to the Other. Buddhist forms of spirituality, as was noted earlier, seek to overcome desire. The goal of Hindu spirituality is to become one with Brahma, the Infinite. The process is to lose the self in the great Self.

Because, in biblical understanding, God is personal and individuated, human beings, "made in the image of God" (according to the biblical phrase), are also individuals. A deep level of spirituality can only be achieved by persons who have a realistic understanding of the self, or, in the common phrase, a "good self-image." Put the two ideas together, and we are talking about the image of God and the image of self.

The theological roots of spirituality are the awareness of who God is and how God acts, insofar as humans can perceive this.

The biblical roots of spirituality are to be found in the descriptions of how people who knew God were related to him in their lives. The psychological roots of spirituality pertain to how individuals today understand themselves in order to grow in relationship to God.

"Who am I?" is not an easy question to answer because it brings all kinds of discomfort. A person can reflect on life by writing an autobiography. Such writing could be concrete—if not completely objective—concentrating on dates and events. One need not bare the soul in order to write such a document. A more candid approach would be to write a memoir. This is subjective, and may be more revealing than is the concrete autobiography. Memories include the feelings evoked by events and other people. It is said that every experience in life becomes incorporated into the person, however deeply the memory may be hidden. People remember only memories they can cope with, and usually these are the good memories. All the potential for the self may be present at conception, but the development of the self is determined by life experiences. In order to know the self, it is necessary to recall the past. Journal-keeping has been a way in which people have been doing this for centuries. John Wesley's journal preserves the story of his eighteenth-century British itinerant ministry, as well as reflections on his work and his journey in faith. John Wesley's American contemporary John Woolman also produced a journal that provides glimpses into what it meant to be a witness to Christian faith as a member of the Society of Friends in the pre-Revolutionary colonies.

A diary is a more specific type of journal-writing in which daily events and thoughts are recorded. Written at the close of each day, the diary has a sense of immediacy unmatched by any other form of writing. The authenticity of all such personal writing depends on the degree of unselfconsciousness with which it is written. Some diarists display a knack of recording for posterity.

The answer to the question "Who am I?" is the self, which

incorporates all the past—including the past of one's family, culture, religion, and national group. This self is acting in the present, and has potential for the future. For many people, this perspective gives a sense of unity and self-confidence. They are able to affirm the self, understanding both strengths and weaknesses. To be fully the self is to accept imperfection: to know that human beings always show weakness, make mistakes, and deliberately sin. Human beings are not God, but they can become related to God.

Not all people have this positive sense of self. Some have an inordinate need to seem perfect. They can admit no wrongdoing. They can brook no interference. They cannot accept the possibility that another person might equal or even surpass them in some activity. They have mistaken themselves for God. Both the ancient Greeks and the writers of the Bible recognized this trait in some people. The Greeks called it pride (*hubris*), and knew that it leads to a fatal distortion of self-perception. Proud people have no need for the spiritual life. They see themselves as already divine!

At the other end of the spectrum are those who believe themselves to be of no worth. Timid and hesitant, they go through life looking in all directions, measuring themselves against others and finding themselves wanting. This sense of unworthiness interferes with growth in the spiritual life. They feel too sinful to aspire to any awareness of the Holy One. In times past, such people haunted the confessional, hoping with each new assurance of forgiveness that they would be free. But the need was an inner one. Their "sins" as wrongful acts were really few, having importance only in their own eyes. Their "sins" or sinfulness was in being unwilling (or unable) to receive the redemption offered by God, to accept freedom in the Spirit, and to put on the new person in Christ.

Self-awareness as a human being includes having a good sense of self, without claiming the wholeness of God, and being freed from a sense of unworthiness that prevents one from seeing the self as a child of God. These are psychological insights but they have theological connotations. They describe people in relation to God. Recall how the psalmist says in one place, "I am reckoned among those who go down to the Pit" (Ps. 88:4); and in another place affirms, "I will sing of thy steadfast love, O Lord, for ever" (Ps. 89:1). God yearns for the people of Israel when they are in bondage. Jesus longs to gather the people of Jerusalem as a hen gathers her chickens to protect them. The affirmative sense of self is matched by the joyful assertion of being made in the image of God.

Spiritual development can also emerge from the quest for certainty. The nature of the quest indicates that one begins from a sense of uncertainty. The idea of search is philosophical, theological, and also psychological. A person who is unsatisfied looks for security. Human relationships sometimes are explored this way. As two people learn about each other, they know whether to trust each other, and whether to risk their lives with each other.

So it is with the spiritual life. Knowing about God involves no risk. Trusting God involves the risk of one's life. As the classical mystics knew, the uncertainty can become deeper the longer one is involved in the life of the Spirit. Only by patient waiting upon God is one delivered from the darkness. We dare not overlook the psychological dimensions of the mystic's life. Some were prone to extremes of emotion: one day in the height of ecstasy; at another time in deep darkness. Their psychological makeup seems to have been part of their spiritual calling. Some people, because of their particular emotional and intellectual makeup, have a unique ability to surrender themselves to God, to have an overwhelming sense of the presence of God, and to feel a certainty of God unmatched by any human relationship. They also face the possibility of feeling abandoned; of living in the depths of despair while waiting for the action of God to lift them up.

Other people live on a more equable level. They love God, but not ecstatically. They respond to God, but need a rational foundation that makes sense to them before committing their lives to the direction of another—even God. For such people to trust God they need to be shown. "Doubting Thomas" is a psychological and spiritual prototype of many persons.

Psychological understandings are helpful in interpreting why people act as they do. This is not to say that *post mortem* psychoanalyses can be made with assured accuracy, although Erikson's portraits of Luther and Gandhi are impressive evidences of the psychologist's skill. The insights of Freud have helped many individuals to probe the depths of their being, if only to accept the fact of an inner life hidden even from themselves. Freud's was a humanizing voice in a culture that believed in progress toward perfection. By differentiating among three aspects of the self (our personal trinity!), Freud helped people accept the past hidden deep within them; the self that they see and know every day; and the sublimated self or "superego," which governs personal morality and may be either helpful or hurtful. A spiritual life is built on an acknowledgement of the existence of the full self and a willingness to become integrated as a person.

Currently the writings of C. G. Jung are newly influential among people studying spiritual growth. Jung was more aware of the spiritual dimension of life than were many analytical psychologists of the early twentieth century. He asserted that in addition to the individual unconscious there is a collective unconscious made up of the myths and images of the racial past. These are archetypes, patterns with a universal character expressed in acts and images, and they appear in dreams. An awareness of the meaning of this collective past will help people achieve individuation in their personal lives, the sense of personhood. Jung was interested in the psychology of religion, saw a need for people to develop the spiritual side of life, and faced this question in his book *Modern Man in Search of a Soul* (1933).[2]

Ann Belford Ulanov[3] has built on Jungian insights in developing her approach to the spiritual life. Morton Kelsey has followed Jung's theory on dreams and, observing that the Bible is filled with stories of dreams as the expression of God's self-revelation, has developed a praxis for helping people use their dreams in the development of the spiritual life.[4]

Abraham Maslow coined the phrase "self-actualization."[5] Speaking to the subject of self-awareness and self-fulfillment, he developed a "ladder" of needs. The fulfillment of each need, he suggested, leads to the quest to fulfill the next one, until a person achieves complete fulfillment, which is self-actualization. Practical needs come first; until a person is fed and clothed, it is impossible to think of emotional fulfillment, and until that is accomplished one does not seek spiritual fulfillment. The idea of a "ladder" in spiritual development is ancient; it is found in the Kabbalah and in the writings of medieval Christian mystics. Maslow replaces the progressivist idea of completion with that of fulfillment, and concentrates on self-development. His is a secular approach to spiritual development, but some of the human needs he outlines are common to all people.

One further psychological root of the spiritual life is to be found in the study of extrasensory perception. Begun in England with the establishment of the Psychical Society in 1881 and extended to Cambridge, Massachusetts, a few years later, its members have always sought to be intellectually professional in seeking grounds for demonstrating the reality of unusual phenomena. They begin with the hypothesis that the concrete objective phenomena that can be tested through current scientific criteria are not the only existent phenomena. Thoughts seem to have a life of their own and can be transferred from person to person beyond the known boundaries of space and time. Clairvoyance, telepathy, and precognition are among the phenomena studied. Because psychical investigators deal with an alleged reality beyond that of the senses, they have something in common with all who seek to develop the spiritual life.[6]

Education for Spiritual Growth

One basic way to help people develop spiritually is to probe theological insights. Usually the study of theology has taken a cognitive approach as primarily an intellectual discipline. How people understand God intellectually is vital to any acceptance or rejection of relationship to God. The spiritual dimension is developed as people become aware that the reality of God is important for them. A philosophy of religion attempts to develop rational answers as to how and why God exists. The spiritual dimension opens a yearning toward One who is beyond the self, foundational to human existence and to the created universe.

An understanding of the meaning of revelation can be taught. People may become aware that God is present in the world but they do not usually probe the reasons why they know this, or inquire as to the nature of revelation. Yet revelation is a basic area for theological inquiry. For some people revelation is concrete, and is to be found in the words of the Bible narrating God's activity and telling God's Law. To others, revelation is insight into the nature of the activity of God interpreted through the words of the Bible. In particular, the Bible witnesses to the Word of God in Jesus Christ. Spiritual development depends in part on the understanding of how God is revealed in the natural world, the Bible, and, for Christians, through Jesus Christ.

Those seeking to mature in the spiritual life will also need to learn about the relationship between the seeking of God and the seeking of humans for God. What is the meaning of the divine initiative? Does God seek all people? Are some paths to God more acceptable than others? Why are some people able to respond to the divine initiative while others seem content to live without God? In another dimension, what sets people on the search for God? An educational process awakens both a desire to know God and a curiosity to seek knowledge about God.

For Christians the understanding of God is made complicated by the description of God as Trinity. If education is designed as a cognitive experience, efforts will be made to harmonize the threefold nature of God with the fact that there is one God. However valid the approach may be for intellectual understanding, this will not be a satisfying help in the development of the spiritual life. God as Creator, Redeemer, and Sanctifier evokes a sense of mystery and wonder. Rather than being a form of divine arithmetic, the understanding of Trinity points to the impossibility of domesticating the Eternal One through human analogies. Teaching a dynamic interpretation of God as Trinity is a challenge that educators have yet to meet, concerned so frequently as they are with product more than with process.

Theological insight as a path to spiritual awareness can best be found within the religious community. In addition to providing intellectual content, the church gives an added dimension by being a community through which believers can communicate their faith to other people.

For this reason, education in the spiritual life is enhanced through worship. Differing forms of worship encourage different forms of spirituality Pentecostals have a sense of the action of the Holy Spirit through their worship, which is communicated through constant encouragement to individuals to share their concerns and feelings; to pray and praise God individually and simultaneously; to witness in the company of others both in thanksgiving and repentance.

Another form of worship might express the sense of Transcendence through the shape of the building, liturgical appointments, more measured forms of music than those of Pentecostals, and a more closely structured liturgy. The shape of spirituality is defined by a service of worship. Some liturgies bring to the worshippers a sense of the immediacy of God. Others cultivate the feeling of awe and transcendence. Each form shapes the spirituality of its adherents.

The Bible is integral to the development of the spiritual life.

Education in the Christian and Jewish traditions includes learning the stories of biblical people. Hearing and understanding stories has no age limitation. The Bible began as an oral tradition. When the stories are vividly told, people of all ages, children as well as adults, relive the lives of its people. Their problems are human problems; their needs are human needs. The boy Joseph, in his egotism, mirrors adults as well as children. The man Joseph, facing a decision for reconciliation, is in a situation that both children and adults have experienced. Reflection on the stories and theological interpretation will await an age when the mind is ready to reason abstractly, but the Bible is not a philosophical document. It does not deal with abstractions but with real situations between God and human beings. As such, the spiritual insights are available to people of all ages, on a developmental level that each can understand.[7]

Learning how to understand and use the Psalms for spiritual growth is another educational task. People need to become acquainted with the phrases from early years. Children can understand verses from the Psalms long before they grasp the meaning of most biblical stories. Frequently, well-meaning people explain and apply stories in ways that the biblical narrative itself would not substantiate. They do this in an effort to make the Bible "understandable" to children. It would be better to use the Psalms, since all kinds of human needs are expressed in this collection of prayers and hymns. The language of the Psalms should become part of the vocabulary of the believer.

Stories *about* Jesus sometimes fragment the story *of* Jesus. Children and adults study from printed materials intended to help learners understand, interpret, and apply the events of the gospels and the early church. This is good, but it is not sufficient for spiritual development. For this purpose, the reader needs to live the story of Jesus, participate in the life of the earliest Christian community, and walk with Paul in his journeys. Then one can become aware of the power of the Holy Spirit at work in the New Testament story.

Another area of education into the spiritual life is that of contemporary psychology. Whatever or whoever helps us to see ourselves more profoundly as human beings can also help us, through this process, to see ourselves in relation to God. Currently, the work of Ira Progoff, survivor of the Holocaust, has been an aid to the spiritual development of many people.[8] Progoff has developed a particular method of journal-keeping and has trained people to lead workshops. Those involved proceed from introductory to advanced courses. Intensive journal workshops have become a feature in Christian conference centers across the country.

Frank inquiry into the self and one's past can be a help in uncovering the full dimensions of personality, healing the pain of past experiences and relationships, and affirming the essential goodness of a person. Progoff says that he could never have survived concentration camp without self-affirmation in a situation where every effort was made to destroy the self. Journal-keeping can be an aid to the spiritual life insofar as it becomes a way of recording the pilgrimage of one's life with God.

C. G. Jung is pervasively influential in the spiritual quest today. Because the spiritual dimension of life was important to Jung, his writings have seemed to provide psychological authentication for the spiritual quest. Jung's emphasis is on exploring the inner self in order to see the roots of religious yearnings as part of the history of the human race. The question "Who am I?" is set in the context of one's total history as a human being. The memories of community life go farther back in history than do written records, farther than pictures painted or incised into stone. We believe, Jung might say, because human beings have always had a sense of the mystery of the universe, and have always worshipped the Transcendent through some kind of rituals. Mircea Eliade builds on this assertion from an anthropological and philosophical viewpoint, affirming that it is human to ritualize experiences and that the roots of ritual are lost in the mists of time.[9]

This kind of education is not to be cognitively perceived,

although it has intellectual content. This is education leading to the kind of awareness that helps people learn from the human past and feel a continuity with that past. Jung points to the importance of symbols, a concept that is often difficult for the "average" Protestant but intrinsic to the experience of those nurtured in the so-called liturgical churches, whether Catholic, Orthodox, Anglican, or Lutheran. The whole question as to whether old symbols can be filled with meaning for those who have hitherto ignored them, or whether new symbols, having no past, can be given meaning, is an idea demanding reflection. Jung is concerned with interior symbols and symbols of the human past, but the inquiry spills over into the symbols developed by religions now being practiced around the world. Jung himself made use of the mandala, a symbol more frequently used in Eastern than in Western religion. The word is from the Sanskrit meaning "circle," and the mandala represents the universe, with God at the center. The human effort is the concern to enter the circle and seek the Divine. When Jung found that his patients would draw forms of mandalas to represent their dreams, he came to the conclusion that the mandala was an archetypal symbol. Encouraging people to become aware of and sensitive to symbols and their meanings and to apprehend dreams, along with the potential spiritual dimension of dreaming, are areas through which education in the spiritual life can be enriched. For that reason the contribution toward religious perception and spiritual growth of psychologists such as Jung is invaluable.

7. Nurture in Spirituality

The development of the spiritual life includes both education and nurture. Its cultivation requires awareness of the way people grow mentally and emotionally throughout the human life span.

Developmental Needs and Spiritual Nurture

The assertion of an innate yearning toward God or an inborn capacity for religious development, although unproven, has been made by a number of writers. As a philosophical concept, it found expression in the "religious feeling" discussed by nineteenth-century theologian Friedrich Schleiermacher. More recently the psychological approach of James W. Fowler has been popular. Fowler builds on the studies of Erikson and Piaget to outline stages of faith development. He states in the preface of his book a belief that faith is a human universal: "We are endowed at birth with nascent capacities for faith. How these capacities are activated and grow depends to a large extent on how we are welcomed into the world and what kinds of environments we grow in."[1] All people who deal with the religious development of families, churches, or synagogues would seem to assume such a premise. The position taken is that positive intervention by believers into the lives of their small children is expected to result in spiritual growth.

The developmental psychologists give some clues as to the direction such intervention might take. When Erik Erikson writes that a primary need of infants under the age of two is for nurturing, he is stating a thesis with theological overtones.

Through nurturing, he says, the infant develops the capacity to trust; or, conversely, will grow up mistrusting the self and others.[2] Trust is close to "having faith." Thus, by implication, the first step in the development of the spiritual life is to surround an infant with people who nurture the child so lovingly that the child is able to trust the environment.

As soon as a child begins to understand words, believing parents will frequently spend a moment at bedtime referring joyfully to the spent day's events, speaking of God, and in a connecting gesture softly touching the child's hands or head. The first words of prayer do not have the meaning they would have for adults. They are simply a symbol that links the child, the nurturing person, and that Presence who has been named God. God becomes connected with rest, quiet, security, and joy—all good experiences.

In some families it is a custom to give thanks at meals. In Jewish homes there is a special home liturgy to welcome the Sabbath on Friday evening. The mother lights the Sabbath candles with a prayer of thanksgiving. The father blesses the glass of wine. In this concrete ceremony, even the youngest child becomes aware that someone not visible is being addressed with joy, and that a special event is being celebrated.

Jean Piaget has described this age, when the child is beginning to comprehend the meaning of words, as the sensor motor stage.[3] Actions of this kind, perceived by the child but not verbally explained to the child, are the earliest forms of learning offered by a social group; in this instance, by the family.

Somewhat later in the developmental process, the two- and three-year-old child is developing a sense of autonomy, to use Erikson's terminology. Children at this age want to make some decisions for themselves. When they join in the structured worship events of a family, they need to be persuaded, not coerced. Decision and commitment are terms used in speaking of later religious development, but the ability to make decisions begins at this early age. Some people, even as adults, have trouble speaking for themselves, and find it difficult to make personal commitments. The child who does not develop autonomy experiences a sense of doubt or shame.

Children from the ages of two through five are, in what Piaget calls a pre-operational stage. He characterizes this as a time when motor activity is important and children seek concrete explanations for the things they experience. Children develop the spiritual life when they are invited to participate in significant religious events such as Christmas and Easter. Commonly, children are introduced to Christmas through the magic of Santa Claus, the concreteness of the baby in a manger, and the general air of excitement in the giving and receiving of gifts. To adults, who may make the Advent pilgrimage through gospel passages recounting the announcement to Mary, the proclamation of John, and the eschatological message, Christmas can become an awesome event, celebrating the entrance of God into human existence in the lowly birth at Bethlehem. Young children do not understand theology, but they soon develop a sense of wonder. They may give concrete explanations to supernal events, but they also sense the expectation of the season, the joy of celebration, and the stillness that can come on Christmas Eve. If Christmas is a spiritual experience for adults, it will be so for small children who live in such an environment. The joy of Easter is communicated similarly, not through verbalized explanation, but in the beauty that surrounds the liturgy on that day, although our culture tends less to evidence the signs of Easter in homes than it does the signs of Christmas.

While children at this age develop the spiritual life mostly through their actions and environment, they are using words to express needs and feelings toward people. They can express the words of prayer, and they can feel meaning in silence.

Four- and five-year-old children are developing a sense of initiative. Their everyday associations are wide-ranging, beyond their house and into the neighborhood and school. They know the difference between right and wrong, (what is acceptable to authority figures) and many have been taught to connect this authority with God. Whether God is punishing or forgiving depends on the theological stance of family and other teachers, but it is an important factor in juvenile spiritual development. Because the development of the spiritual life is based on a relationship to God, it is important that children feel assured that God is basically loving, and that such a relationship to God should not evoke anxiety.

Children understand the feeling of being alienated from others by wrongdoing and know the steps to reconciliation. The assurance that God forgives and restores (rather than judges) is important in the development of a healthy spirituality.

Another finding by Piaget is that young children believe punishment should fit the amount of wrongdoing and should have no relation to the wrongdoer's intentions. This belief would make a child uncomfortable if he or she were forgiven without punishment. The assurance of having made amends is an important factor in the sense of restoration.

Preschool children are developing a sense of self-awareness. The process is begun when the infant differentiates the self from the mother. It is through the process of individuation that a person can come to know God as a separate Self. Fowler points out also that the child's imagination is developing.[4] Stories from the Bible and religious observances are important, but adults must not expect children to understand these either cognitively or spiritually on an adult level.[5]

Erikson, like Freud, reminds us that children at this age level are evolving new relationships to parental figures. It is unavoidable in the Christian context not to use the term "Father" in reference to God, because it is used in the Lord's Prayer, which children frequently learn at this age. Undoubtedly the child internalizes the experiences of a male parental figure, but it is also possible that an "ideal" father figure emerges, whatever meanings the human figure might convey. Andre Godin, studying the effect of this image on adults, indicates both the internalization and change that take place across the years.[6] Except for this usage in the Lord's Prayer, it is possible to use only the name of God, with whatever qualifier seems appropriate in a situation and without pronouns or symbolic terms. This is the basic way through which growing children can appropriate for themselves an understanding of God that is not gender-oriented.

The school-age child develops spiritually from experiences of the earlier years. If time has been cultivated for brief moments of silence, the child will be able to appreciate stillness as a way of becoming aware of the presence of God. The sense of joy and wonder felt in response to the natural world experienced by the child brings to consciousness a God who was "in the beginning." This connection is made when people who believe have been affirming God the Creator within the family or the church since the child first began to understand words. A sense of the transcendent and immanent presence of God becomes part of life experience.[7]

School-age children also wrestle with doing right and doing wrong, with justice and injustice, or—in their terms—what is fair or unfair. Children who have learned dependable relationships through family and friends are developing a spirituality through which to understand the biblical insight that God is just. They can begin to accept the reality of injustice and to know, like the psalmist, that although life may not always be fair, one can have hope, because God is righteous. With their sensitivity to intentions, they are more keenly aware of unjust treatment when *what* they have done is counted more important by some adults than *why* they have done something. Understanding the biblical assertion of the grace of God is difficult unless grace has been a factor in the child's growing spiritual life and the relationship to God.

In this stage of concrete thinking, during which children find satisfaction in the accomplishment of concrete tasks, one should not look for the kind of spirituality adults imply when they use the word "spiritual." Children love God with the same matter-of-fact quality with which they approach other relationships. This very emphasis on the concrete may lead religious education teachers into settling for knowledge *about* the Bible that makes scripture a mundane recital of events. This is a time when the skill of storytelling is an important medium through which to help young learners glimpse the sense of mystery in biblical events. Older children are beginning to turn from acquiescence to the questioning of religious statements. Attempts to meet questions with a rational approach may only make the biblical story seem illogical. Older boys and girls have not caught the inner meanings that sustain adult interpretations. It would be better for adults to say to a child, "I do not completely understand this either," or "God is acting in this event, but I do not know how." The child may not become convinced, but the adult has not been boxed into an intellectual position that could not be sustained later when an adolescent will ask more questions. Older children can begin to understand the significance of festival seasons such as Easter and Christmas, which go beyond the story and even beyond the cultural celebrations, whether these be Christmas trees or Easter eggs.

Some older children are sensitive to the presence of God in a personal way that calls forth a response of faith. This is the age level at which many churches have encouraged children to make a commitment of faith. The child does this in all sincerity. In particular, the figure of Jesus frequently has a personal appeal. The response has been to see the self in the gospel story, called as the disciples were called, feeling a nearness to the gracious presence of Jesus in Galilee, who called the children, healed the sick, and assured people of God's love and care. Prayer takes on a new dimension and God may be present to them in a deeper way than earlier. They may find the nearness of God comforting when they have done wrong or have been wronged, when school is difficult, or if they feel misunderstood at home. Faith has become personal.

Edward Robinson, writing from the Religious Experience Research Unit at Manchester College, Oxford, offers anecdotal information from his research to bring a further dimension to the study of children's religion. Protesting that "developmentalism (i.e., Piaget, Kohlberg, and Fowler) has become the dominant school of thought underlying the contemporary religious education theory," he wants to make it clear that these theories, while having value and relevance, are not exhaustive. In fact, they are limited by their basic assumption that "children are incapable of experiencing, perceiving, or thinking as mature adults." The intuitive quality of spiritual development is demonstrated by the remembrances by adults of moments of transcendence that came to them as children and indelibly stamped their later religious experiences.[8]

Many years ago, Lewis J. Sherrill, while professor of religious education at Union Theological Seminary in New York, wrote a book entitled *The Struggle of the Soul*.[9] In the book he relates that Kirkegaard had said that God met people in times of deep need, because when life was going well, they felt no need of God. Sherrill reaffirms that in the psycho-social crises of life (Erikson's phrase), because of the uncertainty of the situation, people are more likely to be open to an awareness of God. The six-year-old, having dealt with the tasks of achieving some measure of trust, autonomy, and initiative, is tempted to stay in that comfortable preschool equilibrium rather than to face the tasks in the school age looming ahead. One film pictures a six-year- old taking an enormous first step into the school bus, which, from the child's perspective, is a cavernous vehicle.[10] This is a new world, socially and psychologically speaking, and the child needs help—supernatural help, one might say. The child at this age is more open to the relationship with God (or is open in a new way) than would have been possible two years earlier or might be two years later.

Developmental Needs of Adolescence

The turn to adolescence presents a similar situation. There has been a kind of equilibrium during the years from six to twelve. Now, all at once, there are physiological and emotional changes, at the same time that new kinds of social and educational demands are being made through school and family. It is an exciting—but also an anxious—time. Erikson sets the task here as one of achieving a sense of identity. "Who am I?"—not in relation to the family—but to the adolescent's own generation; and not only to the peer group but to individual uniqueness.[11]

For some, religious faith has been an extension of the family environment. Now other environments become important. Some young people leave the religious practices of the church, despite any supportive effect adults may have hoped for from early confessions of faith. They may still be religious and have a deep sense of the spiritual. They may experience faith through prayer, the natural world, or friendships. Powerful sexual responses become channels for the libido, which used to find an outlet in love for God and through forms of worship. Some adolescents in the process of individuation find strength in an individual relationship to God, developing a personal spirituality which could become a long-term pattern.

Seeing life as vocation, and therefore as a spiritual experience, usually happens, if it does, during late adolescence. Youthful idealism infuses life with energy, hope, and dreams. Bringing the whole life into relationship with God is the mark of a maturing spirituality. Many who will eventually choose church vocations make that decision during this time.

The crisis element in the adolescent experience of ego development leaves them open to seek support. It might seem tempting to stay within the protected environment of later childhood, but there is also the urge to try independence, whatever the risks. The Bible makes the paradoxical assertion that true freedom is to be found not in self-will, but in seeking the will of God. The only really independent people are those who are able to be interdependent, and even to acknowledge a need for dependence in some situations. Until a person has a sure sense of autonomy and personhood, it is impossible to develop this kind of freedom. For this reason, some people who study the rite of confirmation believe that the promises of commitment it exacts can only be made in late adolescence or young adulthood.[12] When this kind of freely willed response can be made, it signifies well for the beginning of a mature spirituality.

Developmental Needs of Adults

Adults also live through stages. The Bible describes such stages in the Book of Proverbs. So does Shakespeare. Analysis of specific tasks at each stage results from the contemporary penchant for orderly description. Erikson's three stages now have been supplemented by Levinson's transitional stages, bringing the total to six.[13]

A person who has been developing spiritually through childhood and adolescence will continue to grow. The assurance of being fully oneself in the presence of God enhances the possibility of building on selfhood in the choice of work and the early relationships of adulthood.[14] The choice to stay in the home environment or move to another geographical or sociological locale tests the self-image. Like Jacob, sent away from home, young adults can feel strengthened by the assurance that God is present in every place. Choices of marrying or remaining single, of accepting a vocation that includes celibacy or choosing the person one will marry—these are both opportunities and crises in young adulthood. They are not a basis on which a spiritual path is chosen, but rather one through which the chosen path is strengthened.[15]

During late adolescence and early adulthood, the change into a totally different religious group may be made. In recent years, adherents to the Hare Krishna movement, Buddhist groups, and the Unification Church frequently have come from this age group. There is some yearning for a satisfying spiritual life that these young adults are not finding in the established churches and synagogues from which they have come. They did not choose the route of secularity. They sought and found a different kind of spiritual environment that demanded of its adherents a dedicated and distinctive lifestyle.[14]

The middle years bring other stresses. Young adults have a dream of success, but ten or fifteen years later have to readjust their view as to what constitutes success. This is basically a spiritual problem. For those in the Christian tradition, following the way of the Cross is not a success-oriented vocation. There could be conflict between the spiritual quest and the goal of success, whether social, financial, or vocational. A person might be tempted to avoid the spiritual side of life completely in order to still the questions.

The young adult dream becomes tarnished at another point: marriage is not perfect. The effort at developing individuality while cultivating mutuality may not have resulted in an ideal family. Moreover, children, where present, may seem to exhibit an awkward ability to be like their parents in the worst possible ways! Guilt becomes a factor when extreme stress occurs between couples who viewed their marriage as a sacrament, with promises made and blessed in the presence of God and witnessed to by a supportive congregation. The stresses of marriage can strain spiritual development. A person may try to avoid self-examination, or see the self mirrored in Bible and liturgy. If a marriage dissolves, a sense of guilt may become stronger, and a feeling of abandonment by God, or an avoidance of God, may occur. Conversely, those couples who have found mutual fulfillment in marriage may find in the spiritual life that God seems to be an intruding third person. Who needs God when all is going well? Others see the love of God mirrored in the love of the spouse, and forge a form of spirituality that grows out of their life together.

The middle years also bring involvement with the broader world. Being caught up in the problems of the society in which one lives cannot be avoided, unless a person makes a deliberate effort to do so. Newspapers and television bring a confrontation between contrasting lifestyles: refugees are seen by those who live in settled neighborhoods; the unemployed are in the view of those with secure jobs; war-torn villages impinge on peaceful towns; hunger is set alongside affluence.

It is possible to retreat into a private spirituality, affirming to oneself that if everyone had a good relationship with God, no one would oppress anyone else, and those who were in trouble would have spiritual resources with which to meet the need. Another response would be to avoid religious experience on the basis that there seems so little correspondence between religious faith and the alleviation of human suffering. A synthesis toward a mature spirituality is made by those who can accept the world's suffering while actively working for amelioration in whatever ways they deem acceptable. Their spiritual roots are in the prophets of Israel and Luke's gospel. Spirituality in the middle years does not have the warm glow that might have been possible in adolescence, and is long past the innocent wonder of childhood devotion. These persons can begin to feel something of the agony of God. The suffering of Israel has meaning. The suffering of Christ has power. Redemption takes on new meaning.

Older adults must face their own mortality. In the world's eyes, they have passed the peak. Conversely, they are at a vantage point from which to view life in a broad perspective. Some of life's goals have been fulfilled; some of the tasks completed. They have made accommodation to unachieved ambitions. Serenity rightfully belongs to age. There should be a sense of having become fully a person. This is a time for recognizing that death is near: more years have been lived than will be lived. For people who have achieved this life-view, spirituality becomes a deepened relationship to God. An awareness of the eternal and transcendent becomes their source of hope at transition between life and death. Other people withdraw from active life; some may long for halcyon years that will never return, or may view life with regret for accomplishments unfulfilled. Some people look to the future with fear or bitterness. They may even be so paralyzed by the desire for stability as to be unable to make the necessary decision to change to a lifestyle more consonant with their age. Old age is a time when people either feel at one with God or abandoned by God. If the contrast sounds shocking, remember that it is stated from the human side. Those great practitioners of the spiritual life who have given us an example sometimes felt separated from God, but never abandoned. Whatever cultivation of the spiritual life has been made through the years will bear fruit most fully now. Only the old can share the perspective of God as they survey several generations in family and society. Acceptance and serenity are marks of the final maturing of a spirituality that can affirm "Not my will but thine be done" and "It is accomplished."

Spiritual Nurture in Community

The spiritual life is nurtured within community. This does not require living a dedicated life within an enclosed community, although that style has nurtured a deep spirituality for the few who have elected it. For most people life "in the world" is their existence. Their spiritual life develops within the parish congregation. Some congregations seem better able to nurture the spiritual life than do others. This has nothing to do with the size of the congregation. A small membership can be loving and caring, or it can become ingrown and unwelcoming. A large congregation can be impersonal, especially in cities or suburbs where people move in and out of it frequently. Or it can become a matrix for the development of nourishing groups, inviting people in accordance with their needs. The ability of a congregation to nurture also depends on the spiritual gifts of its members. The presence of God seems to radiate through some people into the lives of others, so that they are a transforming element in the life of any parish.

Pastors can be instrumental for growth in the spiritual life of a congregation when spirituality is an important element in their own lives. The kinds of activity frequently expected of clergy are not conducive to the cultivation of the spiritual life.

Like their parishioners, pastors spend the day following a schedule laid out by the office appointment book. Those in small membership churches may spend many afternoons making visits that will gladden hearts by sociability, but for various reasons may not enrich the religious lives of either pastor or parishioner. This is not to say that all visits should advance the spiritual life. A pastor can encourage people who desire to grow in their spiritual life to find others with whom to share the quest.

Pastors sometimes assume (do their parishioners also?) that time spent at the office is only for transacting church business. They feel guilty if they take time for reading, study, and meditation. Yet this may be the most important "business" that they transact for their congregation. The continuing spiritual development of the pastor may be more important to the life of a parish than is most other work. Asked to rank the importance of the functions of clergy, many congregations will put preaching high on the list. They may little realize that the quality of preaching is partly dependent on the time spent in biblical study, general reading, meditation, and prayer. The quality of counseling a minister is able to offer is also enriched by spiritual depth.

People have differing gifts. Some have a gift for administration and by developing parish life use this gift to the fullest. Others find their gift in educational work, and this becomes a focus in the parish. For others the gifts may be in preaching, liturgy, or counseling. People need to become aware of the gifts their clergy have, in order to know where to encourage that development and where gifts need to be supplemented by the gifts of other members. Clergy speak with gratitude of laity who have ministered to them through spiritual gifts, and of members whose lives have strengthened the life of the parish. Cultivation of the spiritual life of a parish is enhanced when all minister to one another.

Teachers in the congregation also nurture spirituality. Most parishes have a religious education program for all ages, from infants through older adults. Some people will teach because they were asked and could not refuse. Many of these grow in their commitment. Others feel an initial call to teaching. They may be skilled in biblical interpretation, concerned about social issues, or practiced in interpersonal relationships. Some will be people of deep spirituality. This quality will influence what and how they teach. It may not make any perceptible difference in the content or method, but the relationship to God will be communicated between teacher and class. This interaction has been the key factor in the process of Christian commitment for many people.

For these reasons everything that happens at every age level is important for nurturing spirituality. In the earlier section, the emphasis was on the family's role in the developmental process for children and young people. The church also has a specific role.[16]

Parents bring infants to the church nursery while they attend church. This nursery is more than a babysitting effort. The love and concern of the person in charge carry a silent message to the infant of the nurturing love that makes faith possible. The first step of the spiritual life is taken here. Whatever nurturing is given in the family can be continued during this one hour each week. Even when nurturing is lacking in a family it should be offered here. The amount of time spent is not important; the quality is.

Those who teach young children are also nurturing their pupils' spiritual life. Verses of scripture remind children of God's unfailing love and care, invite them to stillness, and assure them of forgiveness. The teacher's own experience of God is communicated to the children. They accept as true that which is shown them by someone in whom they trust. The teacher of children becomes their spiritual guide.

Teachers of school-age children further the dimensions of spiritual growth by continuing the use of prayer, scripture, and personal experience. School-age children (grades 1–6) begin to identify with biblical people. The perspective from which biblical stories are told is important. Be aware of the sensitivity people such as Moses, Elijah, and Jeremiah had in hearing and responding to God. Help children see how the deep relationship between God and Jesus was the foundation of his ministry of healing and teaching. Show children how God strengthened people in times of need. You will want children to know that people in Bible stories were human like us. They sinned, resisted God, called on God, and responded to God. Do not idealize biblical people. This destroys the power they can have to bring others an awareness of God. Children at this age level can become engaged in prayer together, remembering before God those who are absent, in need, and in joy. They can be encouraged (but should never be required!) to voice their petitions during a few moments of quiet. The use of a response by the whole group after each prayer is affirming: "We pray you, O God," or "We thank you, O God."

Spiritual development during adolescence demands more thought and inquiry by those who work with young people. Too often the emphasis in published studies has been on youth programming. Turning from one psycho-social stage to another, as has been said earlier, is a crisis point, and a nexus at which God can enter a life. Adolescents, poised between childhood and adulthood, may be deeply sensitive to the spiritual dimensions of life. They are aware of this in their developing sexuality, in their yearnings toward the future, and in their questions about the purpose of life. Because they are developing the capacity to think abstractly, they can evade spiritual issues by forming ideas *about* God or defining life's purposes. Such intellectual efforts may seem more comfortable than admitting doubt and struggling in the process of forming a mature faith. God is with them in the process, and the adolescent, becoming aware of the divine Presence, can be helped by the guidance of a teacher who is sensitive to both the spiritual side of life and to the needs of young people. This can be a critical time in spiritual development. During late adolescence, many who go into religious vocations or other forms of human service will make that decision. They will see in this decision a way of expressing their relationship to God if they have been encouraged by someone who has this perspective.

The whole life of a congregation nurtures the spiritual development of children and youth, but may assist that of the adults in special ways. This attitude is most strikingly exhibited by the treatment of new people in the community and the congregation. Many churches give a courteous welcome, exchanging names and sometimes (but not always) making sure that visitors are made comfortable at the ubiquitous coffee hour. After that, newcomers may be left to find their own way. A spiritually discerning parish, or even a small group or a few individuals will be drawn to new people, discovering the spiritual gifts that they have to bring to the congregation. People come new to a church hoping to be spiritually strengthened. The attitude of the congregation toward newcomers gives the answer.

A congregation also demonstrates the quality of spiritual life by concern for each other. People may be totally indifferent; wrapped up in their personal lives and various friendship groups. Other congregations are open and responsive. For example, when there is illness in a family, someone organizes a group to bring hot food to the whole family each evening during the emergency. Others set up a schedule for helping at home, driving children to church, shops, or doctor appointments. This is spirituality at work. When there is the pain of bereavement, divorce, or unemployment, people are there to help—or understandingly to stand aside until help is needed. The spiritually aware are sensitive, and they communicate the caring love of God through their awareness of human need.

This sensitivity to need extends to the wider community. Whether demonstrated in personal acts of lovingkindness to the distressed, or whether the parish sponsors an agency to fill a specific need, such actions are evidence of the spiritual life. Prayer groups nurture spirituality, as well as demonstrate it. Spirituality that eventuates in action indicates commitment to God. The ideal of living for some Christians is to have a warm relationship to their Lord. They identify with the disciples who spent time alone with Jesus to hear his words. Yet to these disciples Jesus said, "As you did it to one of the least of these my brethren you did it to me." The reference was to that eschatological time when true commitment would be demonstrated by feeding the hungry, clothing the naked, and visiting those in prison. The expansion of Christian faith around the world is also evidence of the spiritual life. This mission has been sustained by groups formed for prayer, study, and giving, in obedience to the command of the Lord to go into all the world.

The life of intercession in any parish is a witness to spirituality. Whether names are listed in a calendar or recited orally at a worship service, these expressions of need and thanksgiving bind the congregation together in the presence of God. These same petitions can be incorporated into the intercessions of small groups and by individuals. How encouraging it can be for a person to know that a congregation prays in this way. All are linked to one another and to God.

Liturgy and Spiritual Nurture

The mode of a congregation's worship is a mark of its spiritual life. There are many forms of liturgy ranging from the simplicity of Quaker worship, where people speak, pray, or sing as they feel moved by the Holy Spirit, to the magnificently ordered liturgy of the Eastern Orthodox churches. Liturgy is never static. Just as it has evolved from its earliest beginnings, of which we have only fragmentary knowledge, so it continues to evolve in each branch of the church around the world. Only recently has the Western church begun to realize that the countries in Asia and Africa need to express their worship in forms different from those brought to them by Christians from Europe and North America. Each form of liturgy has elements that remind worshippers both of the Transcendence of the Holy One, and of the closeness of God in the worshipping congregation. Examine the order of service in any church. There is a balance between words spoken and sung; between those of the minister and those of the congregation; among hymn, prayer, scripture, and preaching. In many traditions the celebration of the Lord's Supper in some form is basic to the congregation's weekly worship.

The individual's devotional life is enriched through participation in the worship of the community. Scripture and sermon should be a source of spiritual growth. Hymns are witness to the faith.

Most people become acquainted with hymns primarily through use in the service of worship. For this reason hymns should be selected with as much attention to words as to music. They can enrich the daily devotional life.

For Advent there is Charles Wesley's great hymn "Come, thou long-expected Jesus." Meditate on the meaning of "expect"—the "feeling" of the word, the sense of eagerness and longing as one looks forward to the coming of the Lord. Think about what it means to be released from fears and sins. Meditate on Wesley's use of hope, desire, joy. Notice that the hymn is a prayer, and conceptualize and use it in that way.

During Passiontide, meditate on Johann Heermann's seventeenth-century hymn "Ah, holy Jesus, how hast thou offended, that man to judge thee hath in hate pretended?" Join in saying. "Who was the guilty? Who brought this upon thee? Alas, my treason, Jesus, hath undone thee. 'Twas I, Lord Jesus, I it was denied thee; I crucified thee." Use the concluding prayer of adoration. This hymn parallels the liturgies for the Sunday of the Passion and for Good Friday in which the congregation, during the reading of the Passion narrative, respond in the words of the crowd to say, "Crucify him." This liturgy ends with an act of adoration: "We adore you, O Christ, and we bless you, because by your holy cross you have redeemed the world."

No hymn better conveys the sense of transcendence than does that from the Liturgy of St. James, found in hymnals as

"Let all mortal flesh keep silence, and with fear and trembling stand; ponder nothing earthly minded, for with blessing in his hand Christ our God to earth descendeth, our full homage to demand." No one has better expressed the inner meaning of the Eucharist than Thomas Aquinas in the hymn that begins "Humbly I adore thee, Verity unseen." He writes, "Taste, and touch, and vision, to discern thee fail; faith, that comes by hearing, pierces through the veil."

Every hymnal has a section of hymns on prayer, the Holy Spirit, and dedication. To neglect the resources of the hymnal is to impoverish the devotional life. Some people will want to sing hymns aloud; others to "sing" them mentally. Some prefer to concentrate entirely on the message conveyed by words. Many tend to think of hymns solely for congregational singing and identify them with particular tunes. Their value lies deeper. Use the hymnal as a devotional resource and explore its richness. Use it for the depth it can give to small-group study. Then hymns will yield their full power of strengthening the spiritual life as part of the liturgy. Those who wrote hymns had distinctive spiritual gifts, their writing extending from the earliest centuries of the church until today. When using hymnody we are linked with practitioners of the spiritual life from many traditions. Each tradition shapes a particular hymnal, but many hymns are used in common, all being resources for spiritual development.

For this reason, the choice of hymns made for the Sunday service is important. You may have noticed how changing a tune will bring a new emphasis to a familiar hymn. Those who choose hymns would do well to remember the extent to which these can be influential and helpful in the development of the spiritual life.

The church year is a continuing way of helping people in spiritual development. From Advent to Pentecost, the Christian community relives the life of its Lord, following the biblical story. During the four Sundays preceding Christmas, the worshippers prepare for this wonderful event, celebrating the entrance of God into human life in the person of Jesus of Nazareth. Lectionary and hymns reinforce the meaning of Advent through their themes. The gospel readings point to the ultimate return of Christ in judgment; John the Baptist who announced his coming, and Mary to whom his coming was first announced. Who are we and where are we in these stories? The spiritual preparation for Christmas contrasts starkly with the everyday preparation in a culture where secular Christmas songs and decorations are combined with shopping to pre-empt a religious season that has not yet come. The many meanings of Christmas to the believer can only become clear through a concentrated effort to be open to God's Spirit during Advent, conveyed through its liturgical mood.

Christmas, as the completion of a time of preparation, is filled with the kind of joy epitomized by the angels' song. This the church has enlarged to become the "Gloria in Excelsis," a hymn of praise to the Incarnate One. The feast of the Nativity concludes with the tradition of the wise men from the East, and Epiphanytide has begun. These are the weeks of his "showing forth." The emphasis in the Eastern churches has been on Christ the Illuminator, and the gospel passages for the season chronicle events to illustrate this, such as the baptism, the wedding at Cana, the calling of the disciples, the teaching from the mount, and the Transfiguration. For those who turn to the gospels for spiritual development, these passages draw them into the presence of Jesus as he showed God's love to people by healing, teaching, calling, and strengthening.

The season of Lent, although a preparatory one as is Advent, has a different tone. We begin to walk the way of the Cross. That is why, during the traditional Ash Wednesday liturgy, worshippers are signed on the forehead with a cross of ash (left from the burning of the previous year's palms) as these words are spoken: "Remember that you are dust and to dust you will return." There can be no resurrection without death. The readings for this season remind us of the foreshadowing of Jesus' death in the gospels: Peter's confession at Caesarea Philippi

("Who do you say that I am?"), the discussion of who would be greatest (places at the right hand and the left, intimating the three crosses), and Jesus' lament over Jerusalem as he viewed the city from the Mount of Olives.

Lent ends with one final week of drama. Palm Sunday is called "The Sunday of the Passion," and we are reminded of the solemnity of the day in the hymn which begins, "Ride on, ride on in majesty; in lowly pomp ride on to die." Palm Sunday is not a day of false expectations but of ironic celebration.

The great three days are Maundy Thursday (named for the new commandment, in Latin *mandatum*), Good Friday, and the Vigil of Easter. Maundy Thursday, with its poignant joy in the celebration of the first Lord's Supper, which was also the Last Supper before the death of Jesus. Spiritual awareness does not come from mournfully dwelling on the day to follow, but on Jesus' promise that he would drink with them in the Kingdom. Paul reminded his hearers: "As often as you eat this bread and drink this cup, you show forth the Lord's death until he comes." We meditate on an eschatological feast.

The stripped altar, darkened church, and silent organ that greet worshippers on Good Friday witness to the utter desolation of the disciples deprived of their Lord. The only response one can make while participating in the reading of the gospel is that of penitence. "Is it nothing to you, all you who pass by?" The question is asked of us also. Not only the Passion narrative, but the simple liturgy of the day can be acts for spiritual strengthening as a person participates with the congregation, and also meditates privately.

Having seen our place in relation to the Cross of Christ, believers are prepared for the joy of Easter Eve: to see the church bright with candles, fragrant with flowers, joyous with organ and voices. As the Lord rested in the tomb, so his people quietly awaited his arising. It is good that baptisms be celebrated at this time: the symbolism of the act becomes clear.

On Easter Sunday, we, like the women, approach the tomb. They represent us, in the simple drama that originated in the medieval English church. The women, seeing the young man in white, are startled. They are asked, "Whom seek ye, Christian women?" and they answer, "We seek Jesus of Nazareth." The answer comes: "He is not here. He is risen. Go. Tell his disciples." The women turn to the congregation and announce the good news: "Christ is risen," to which all respond "He is risen indeed."[17]

Spiritual power can be received at Easter because of the spiritual discipline of Lent. This may have been a discipline of fasting, giving, and other acts of service. It might include prayer and study in groups or individually. It eventuates in meditation on the mystery of the Resurrection in which all the redeemed participate. Through the seven weeks of the Easter season, the appearances of the risen Lord to the disciples are recounted in the lectionary, ending with the gathering on the Mount of Olives at his final appearing before the Ascension.

This leads into the period of Pentecost, the season of the Holy Spirit: six months that celebrate the work of the Christian community in the whole world through the action of the Holy Spirit.

The church year can become a framework to enrich the development of the spiritual life. The lectionary supports this framework biblically. The liturgical traditions also include a collect and a brief prayer that introduces the scripture readings for each Sunday of the year and becomes a meditation on the theme of that day. These are of further aid when one uses a collect thoughtfully, reads the lessons from Old Testament, Psalm, epistle, and gospel, and understands how these are interwoven. So the church has developed the resources of Bible, prayer, and liturgy to help its members in the process of nurture in spirituality.

8. Methods for Spiritual Development

Some people think that because there is a natural quality to the development of the spiritual life, no cultivation is necessary. They forget how Abraham and Moses struggled in the presence of God; how Jeremiah and Amos sought release from their calling; how often Jesus went apart to renew the sources of his relationship with God. Many who have been most understanding of and adept in spirituality have explored and developed suitable methods. Some methods for spiritual development— old yet ever new—will be considered now.

The Practice of Silence and Meditation

Human beings are talkers. We value the person who is an alert conversationalist. We feel awkward when silence falls upon a group. Yet there may come a comfortable silence between two congenial people. For lovers, being together is its own form of expression. Words are unnecessary. Only in silence can they be fully sensitive to each other.

For the same reason, lovers of God have cultivated silence. They have learned that speaking to God in words of prayer can be a way of avoiding intimacy with God. Their own words may make them oblivious to the words God would speak. It is almost impossible to empty the mind of words. They rush in mentally, if not vocally. How then does one hold the mind open?

It is surely not done by trying. When it happens, one will not at first be aware of this. The earliest silence may be a time of reflecting.

Let us begin by thinking about young children. Silence, up to a point, is a game. The teacher says, "Be very quiet while Jane tiptoes around and touches one of you. Can you hear her steps? Do you know when she is close?" Or, cuddling a child, a parent says, "Let's be very quiet while we rock back and forth in the chair. Feel it: forward—back—forward—back." Silence becomes a vehicle for hearing and feeling. Later one says, "Close your eyes and imagine that you are by the shore (or in a meadow). What do you see? What do you hear? What do you feel? What do you smell?" Close your eyes and in silence permit the mind to become projected into another setting, either to recall or to imagine a situation.

Silence can be used when children are learning how to pray at home, or in a church or school setting. This could be introduced by a verse of thanksgiving and praise from scripture. "'Rejoice in the Lord.' What has given us joy today?" Or a verse suggesting quiet: "Let the earth keep silence," or "Be still; know that I am God." This quiet in the presence of God is not an attempt at silencing, as if a person ought not to speak. The purpose is to enhance receptivity. It emphasizes the subjective or "feeling" aspect in worship, which is valid when other elements of worship are also present. Children might be asked to think quietly of how they love God, or feel joy in what God has done, or feel secure because God is with them. They may or may not want to share their thoughts. The minute (which can be gradually lengthened) could end with brief prayer by the teacher. Stillness leads to awareness and intensifies experience. It should not make people feel uncomfortable, but bring relaxation. This observation relates to the experience of silence and not the response that reflection might bring. Sometimes reflection in quiet may lead to discomfort by arousing the impulse to respond by action.[1]

If the practice of silence is begun with small children, as it is among the Society of Friends, the development of silence becomes part of planning for growth in the spiritual life from year to year. The elementary-school-age child may find strength and reassurance from this practice. The focus of silence can grow out of scripture, hymn, or story. Where children have been participating in a project through which they learn about other children in need and plan ways of helping, then in the silence they can both project themselves into the situation, recall what the Bible says, and think in the presence of God of what they can be and do. Out of their meditation can come the beginning of action. Now they are growing beyond the need for inner peace to the need for knowing God's purposes and realizing how they can be part of the fulfillment.

Adolescents need to be with other people and find their identity through peers. Sometimes they need to withdraw from the group. Some may seem to seek solitude because they feel uncomfortable in a social setting. The quiet ones may actually be spiritually aware young people. If silence is not an escape from the realities of human relationships, it can be a strengthening retreat from which to form such relationships. The forms of spirituality used by adults are the forms that adolescents are just beginning to find valuable.

As in other practices of the devotional life, forms of congregational worship offer a pattern for growth. There are traditions in which people expect to enter the church in silence, pray silently, and wait in silence for the service to begin. Some have learned to use the resources of hymnal, Bible, or prayer book as preparatory aids to worship. For them silence is a purposeful time that detaches them for awhile from the hurried pace of everyday life in order that God might be made known to them with new power.

Occasionally, the liturgy provides a place for silence. The bidding prayer guides the intentionality of petitions but leaves a time of silence for individual participation. Silence before or at the close of a pastoral prayer leaves space for the individual worshipper. In those churches where the Lord's Supper is celebrated weekly, people have a long time in silence while the congregation is receiving communion. They may benefit from the suggestion that they meditate on hymn or scripture or pray and listen in silence during this time. Organ or choir music is often offered as a background for the individual's interior silence.

Guidelines given through the worship service encourage people to develop the use of silence when alone. A number of other ways of cultivating the spiritual life through meditation can be learned.

Preparation for meditation is important, and the sequential steps are widely shared across many religious traditions.[2] Meditation is entered via a slow process of relaxation. Although it may seem curious that one can concentrate in order to become relaxed, that is actually the way it is. Begin by thinking of the toes, ankles, and the whole foot. Feel that the earth is holding up one's body: it is not a personal effort. Gradually let the weight drop, especially from places most likely to be taut: hips, shoulders, neck, hands. To relax is to become open, even vulnerable. One is no longer on guard. God can enter. Relaxation is a process of surrender. Contemporary psychiatrist Gerald G. May has this to say about modern people:

> The prevailing cultural attitude of the modern West is that self-image should be as strong as possible. . . .
>
> It is often not until after one has spent the better part of one's life seeking autonomy and self-determination that spiritual awakening occurs, and then it seems one is called upon to reverse the process. Now what is needed is not heroic mastery but the simplicity of becoming as a little child; not self-determination but self-surrender; not self-assertion but dying-to-self.[3]

Dr. May continues by pointing out that the self-image affects spiritual experiences. If one has been taught to control, then to surrender, even to God, becomes threatening. If one's self-image depends upon doing, then passive receptiveness in prayer may be difficult. There is a conflict then between what one has spent many years developing as a person who is part and parcel of the cultural scene and the deeply felt yearning for a spiritual reality that alone can unify life.

If this be the situation, the process of learning how to relax will not be easy, yet it is essential for any openness to God through meditation.

When this preliminary process has been accomplished, body and mind now stilled and focused on the presence of God, there are several ways to continue in the Holy Presence. Many people will use just one verse from scripture. Those who follow a daily lectionary may find their verse from that reading. At this point, they are using scripture as a reminder of being in the presence of God.

The next step is to explore the personal meaning of the verse. This exploration becomes both an intellectual and an emotional exercise. Spirituality includes both dimensions, yet goes beyond either one.

Meditation may concentrate on a person, perhaps a biblical person or one of the guides of the spiritual life whose writings hold personal meaning. Focus on one moment of that person's life. Know that God is present to you as to that person. Be aware of how the presence of God affected that person, and affects your own personhood. There may emerge a word or a direction for you in this mode of contemplation.

Meditate on a scriptural event. Where are you in this event? Be careful not to let this become simply a cognitive or an emotional experience. Many centuries ago, Ignatius Loyola devised a set of spiritual exercises for those who were members of the order he had founded, the Society of Jesus. One of these has been adapted for general use and is widely used today. You are asked to put yourself in the picture at a biblical event—but not to be one of those described in the biblical story. Take, for example, the narrative in which Jesus and the disciples went to the home of a Pharisee for dinner. A woman enters, weeps, washes the feet of Jesus with her tears, dries them with her long hair, and anoints them with fragrant perfume. The gospel does not give reactions from observers except to say that they watched to see what Jesus would do. If you had been present, what might you have said or done? Would you have chosen to maintain silence? What does that mean? Did you choose to speak? To whom would you speak and what would you say? In any such meditative exercise, you are drawn to respond to one or both of the central figures. In the honesty of the response and the willingness to consider more than one response, a person will grow spiritually.

Notice that these are not ways of studying the Bible, but of responding to the Bible in a special way. They are not substitutes for study, exegesis, or asking the meaning of the Bible passage in its time or for this time. The Bible becomes, by this method, a way through which a person today projects backward in time to participate in a biblical event.

The hymnal, spiritual writings, or daily liturgies can also be sources for meditation. But the focus must be on only a few words at a time. Only in silence can God be heard beyond the words.

Meditation may also be an outgrowth of a day's events, or, more precisely, of one event or even one facet of an event. Narrowing down gives focus. The event may call to mind other experiences, or the experiences of other people, biblical situations, words of prayer, or liturgical material. An event may be completely refocused because of time spent relaxed; consciously in the presence of God, allowing new insights to emerge. Similarly a person may focus on the future; its hopes or perils.

Prayer may be the entrance into meditation, by providing either a preliminary focus or a conclusion. In between, the free play of mind and spirit leads into words that convey the meaning of God's word to the self.

Prayer and the Development of Spirituality

The emphasis on meditation is intended to convey an openness to God that does not depend on human thoughts or words.

But spoken prayer is a powerful element in the spiritual life. Writings on this subject have appeared across the centuries and continue to emerge, some having become classics in the devotional life.

"Prayer is not a service of the lips; it is worship of the heart," affirms Abraham Heschel, who sees spontaneity as an important element in it.[4] The problem, he continues, "is not how to revitalize prayer; the problem is to revitalize ourselves." He regards prayer not as a need but as *"an ontological necessity,* an act that constitutes the very essence of man."[5] Heschel movingly expresses this insight in a personal affirmation:

> How much guidance, how many ultimate insights are found in our liturgy.
>
> How grateful I am to God that there is a duty to worship, a law to remind my distraught mind that it is time to think of God, time to disregard my ego for at least a moment! It is such happiness to belong to an order of the divine will.
>
> I am not always in a mood to pray. I do not always have the vision and the strength to say a word in the presence of God. But when I am weak, it is the law that gives me strength; when my vision is dim, it is duty that gives me insight.
>
> Indeed, there is something which is far greater than my desire to pray, namely, God's desire that I pray. There is something which is far greater than my will to believe, namely, God's will that I believe. How insignificant is my praying in the midst of a cosmic process! Unless it is the will of God that I pray, how ludicrous is it to pray.[6]

This passage suggests several things about prayer. One is that God has ordained it. Faith in God and prayer to God are, as it were, gifts of the Holy One. Even the initial impulse, then, is not from the human side. It is not a "work." It further says that prayer is not a matter of mood. This removes communion with God from the area of feelings. If people pray, how- ever "unready," God can do and be for them what is needed. Finally, the passage says that the liturgy leads people to pray. Participating with the congregation, we are carried along in prayer with words not of our own choosing.

People can learn how to pray when the prayer of the congregation or the pastoral prayer includes many elements of approach to God. Such prayer will begin with the needs of the congregation, both corporate and individual, become enlarged to include the life of the whole church, extend to the nation, including its leaders, and conclude with the concerns of all people in this society and around the world. Not every concern can be included in every weekly liturgy, but every area should be called to mind in the presence of God. Congregational prayer, at various points throughout the service of worship, will include praise, thanksgiving, contrition, petition, and intercession. If only praise is included, a congregation does not have to face its failure to live God's intentions. If only individual petition is included, then the needs of other people are ignored; if thanksgiving is the only note, then the concerns of the congregation are neglected.

The importance of congregational prayer lies not only in the kind of worship offered before God on those occasions, but as a model to people in their personal spiritual development. This pattern can be adapted for individual use. These kinds of intentions, rounding out the quiet of meditation or even as a focus for meditation, will enrich growth in the spiritual life.

Increasingly, people are becoming aware of psychological factors in prayer. The work of Jung has influenced many who write about religious experience. None has done so more perceptively than Ann and Barry Ulanov. They define prayer as "primary speech."[7] By this is meant that every wish and every cry for help is prayer. People may address this cry to God, to other people, or to the self. Hence, the primary form of this speech is confession and petition. The language of prayer is nonverbal; it includes images and emotions beyond the conscious level. What happens frequently is that people recognize the primal quality of prayer and, feeling uncomfortable, suppress it, settling instead for words that distort the primary image in an attempt, conscious or unconscious, to pretend with God that things are not what they seem.

Most people would prefer not to probe the psychological roots of prayer, but in avoiding this they may be impoverishing the development of the spiritual life. Particularly in the silence of meditation, these factors come into the forefront. Daydreaming may be a step away from the intentionality of meditation, but to bring fantasy into focus is to bring it into the presence of God. Desires may not seem to be prayers, but when faced openly they may become transformed, and in any event they help people see themselves more fully. If a person accepts the fact that nothing is hidden from God, it would be naive to assume that by brushing aside thoughts one has thereby hidden them.

Children are taught forms of address to God that suggest love and kindness, but other teachings may have left the idea that God also punishes. These conflicting "images" of God are present to them, and until such ambivalence is faced in the Presence of God so that God can be revealed, the spiritual life is impoverished.

People are taught that anger is wrong, so they dare not face their anger, whether toward persons or against injustice, in the presence of God. Yet God alone can help to channel aggression in useful ways.

Sexuality also enters into prayer. On one level, the sexual concerns and attitudes of a person are not far below the conscious level. By bringing these concerns into the presence of God, both the nature of the need and new directions may be discovered. In the writings of some mystics, such as Teresa of Avila, union with God is described in passionate terms that indicate God to be the divine lover who alone satisfies the yearning soul. Many people avoid the sexual aspects of the relationship to God, not willing to see that this too is a gift of God, and that this power transforms all relationships.

People try to pray with their minds, avoiding deep emotional involvement, whether of love or anger, that so permeated the devotion of the great practitioners of the spiritual life. Love is surrender, a waiting and response. Development of the spiritual life includes cultivation of this human quality in relationship to God. There is a dynamic interaction of the human and divine that empowers the new life.

Out of this fully formed spirituality, which enables a person to reveal the full self in the presence of God (God already knowing that self), comes the ability to intercede for others. The Ulanovs write:

> The whole question of who intercedes for whom becomes part of one great current that gathers us into its own course and we begin to experience something of the intermixture of Jesus, the Spirit, and God. We see one God, yet distinct persons. We see that we are distinct persons, yet one, running in the ceaseless flow of God's being in all of us. To pray that God's will be done is to enter and to be increasingly caught up in the current of that will, and to experience an enlargement of our willingness to go forth, to flow, to consent, to correspond. We who thought we were offering prayers of intercession for others come increasingly to realize that the prayers of others—people known and unknown to us, people from the present and from the past, even people in a future yet to come—flow through us and intercede for us. With others and through others we depend upon and accept the flow of God's grace.[8]

From this kind of prayer comes an understanding of what it means to have prayer answered in a way that transcends the specificity that some people seem to ask.

People in the Development of Spirituality

The spiritual life is absorbed as well as taught. It cannot be merely explained. A conscious effort must be made to find persons who themselves understand and are practitioners of the spiritual life as teachers for children and youth. This may seem to ask a lot from believers, but in any congregation there will be some people who show this quality of life. A beginning could be made by providing for teachers an opportunity to explore spirituality with someone well-versed in the practice. By renewing their spiritual life, they will find new insight into the Bible and the worship service. These will then become resources for use with their pupils. While some leaders of children's or young people's groups may have become indifferent to the spiritual side of life, they may also sense a need for renewal as they become more deeply involved in teaching.

Historical figures and contemporary people become exemplars as their stories are told. Biographies, autobiographies, and collected writings bring these people into focus. Although some books are available for children, more need to be written. Each century has its own needs, which may be addressed by contemporaries in ways that convey more meaning than do the writings from the past. Twentieth-century spiritual guides would include Charles de Foucauld and his ministry of reconciliation; Dag Hammarskjöld, whose journal *Markings* revealed a person of spiritual depth engaged in global service; Martin Luther King, Jr., whose "dream" was itself an expression of spirituality; Thomas Merton, a contemplative who developed rapport with counterparts in Buddhist monasteries; Simone Weil, whose searching after God brings a responsive echo from many people; Dietrich Bonhoeffer, whose disciplined spiruality led him into the political scene and eventual death; Basilea Schlink, who founded the Ecumenical Sisterhood of Mary; and Max Thurian, who was one of the founders of the Taizé Community and is remembered for inspiring the Community's reconciling work in postwar France and its continuing international work with young people.

Education for spirituality may be hampered by the agenda that frequently form the core of religious education curricula. Because specific material on predetermined themes has been scheduled for teaching, other material tends to be seen as an intrusion. This attitude is unfortunate. Spiritual models can be incorporated into teaching if the curriculum is designed to permit flexibility and a degree of freedom. When spirituality becomes a subject for brief concentration—as, for example, in a four-week unit of study—the pervasive quality of spiritual growth could be neglected.

When enough individuals in a congregation personify spiritual heritage and practice in their lives, there can develop an ethos that conveys to everyone in the group that "this is the way we live." Particular religious groups have practiced this in specific ways. A specific spiritual ethos can be assumed to exist within the ordered life of a monastic community because those who enter know about the way of life in advance and spend a period of time in preparation, before making a decision to take monastic vows. Particular spiritual practices typify some communitarian groups in which mutual confession and special forms of worship may be ways both of teaching and expressing the spiritual life. But every congregation, by examining its local patterns of worship, can provide enrichment in the spiritual life for its worshippers.

One time in which members of a congregation can cultivate the spiritual life is the interval between entering the church for worship and the opening sentences or hymn. Traditions differ here. In some areas and among some denominations, this is an important time for greeting those who have not been seen during the week and for sharing mutual concerns. For others it is customary to maintain quiet following a moment of silent prayer. Seldom is guidance given by way of suggesting resources for meditation. Yet these moments are an entrance into the presence of God. People have left daily concerns, hoping to receive new strength through congregational worship. Some suggested forms of preparation could be helpful in these instances. The spiritual life is nurtured through times of silence, but people need to be educated as to how to use silence. Aside from a calendar listing the events of the week little may be offered in the church bulletin. Sometimes events in the lives of parish people are announced, and prayer asked for those who are ill. The bulletin might also suggest that worshippers thoughtfully read the hymns, scripture passages (if Bibles are available), or liturgical materials, including responsive readings, in hymnal or prayer book.

Only to the extent that a congregation intentionally helps members cultivate the spiritual life can an ever-deepening spirituality come to characterize the worship, ministry, and mission of that parish and the individual lives of its members.

Spiritual directors must be mentioned among those who nurture the spiritual life. Roman Catholic colleges, seminaries, and monasteries have taken for granted that such a person would be an essential staff member. Protestants have seldom seen spiritual direction as one of the pastoral functions of the minister. Recently, however, there has been a rethinking of the role among Roman Catholics and a consideration of the role among Protestants.

The spiritual director is a person to whom another turns for help along the path of spiritual development. This is someone with whom the personal meaning of prayer can be discussed, the times of dryness and darkness be examined, and perspective brought on the reality of prayer within an individual's life.

Spiritual guidance can be informal—simply an expression of the mutual confidence two people place in one another. James C. Fenhagen writes:

> Although there are times when God addresses us in the midst of solitude, more often than not his address is mediated through people . . . the encounter could be a casual conversation or an experience of great intensity. Whatever the mode, something special happens, as if a door were opened within us, and we are allowed to enter. For a moment we are able to see things differently. There is a burst of creativity or insight that suddenly gives a new dimension to how we think and what we see. Faith tells us that these moments are neither coincidence nor self-induced. They come from outside ourselves in a way that seems to address something deep within us. They are, we believe, an experience of God himself.[9]

The writer continues by stating that one reflects on this process later and the reflection itself becomes prayer.

The spiritual director functions this way, but in a more consistent fashion. Fenhagen prefers to use the term "spiritual guide" or "spiritual companion," because the term "director" gives people the impression that one human being is telling another how to carry out a relationship to God, and that is not possible. The term "guide" suggests that a person has asked for help, and the term "companion" suggests that the guide walks alongside on the path. They are "companions along the way." [10]

The image of life as a spiritual journey has a long tradition. John Bunyan's classic *Pilgrim's Progress* recounts the temptations and victories of a Christian journeying toward the Eternal City. The medieval *Imitatio Christi*, sometimes attributed to Thomas à Kempis, has a section entitled "The Royal Way of the Cross." People from many religious traditions have long made pilgrimages. Jesus and the disciples followed a throng journeying from Galilee to Jerusalem for the Passover. Medieval English pilgrims traveled to Canterbury each spring. Today crowds gather at Santiago de Compostelo in Spain for the festival of St. James the Apostle on July 25. These are brief, concrete times of pilgrimage. But life, too, has been seen as pilgrimage.

The spiritual guide assists persons along the way. Soulfriends can minister to each other. In addition, some people seem to have special gifts for nurturing others in the spiritual life. This becomes a vocation. Through personal conferences with individuals at specific intervals, the spiritual guide listens, counsels, and prays with the person. This process provides boundaries against subjectivity and sentimentality. It tests the intentionality of thanksgiving, contrition, petition, and intercession. The forms of prayer often become clearer through disciplined interaction with a spiritual guide. Contemporary development in the art of spiritual guidance has been enhanced through the recognition of the psychological aspects of personhood.

For those who have the gift, becoming a spiritual guide is a

newly developing ministry. Such "friends" may be lay or ordained, but their role approximates that of a professional func-
tion. Some psychiatrists serve as spiritual directors.[11]

Groups Who Help in Spiritual Development

Perhaps the most immediate group that can assist people to
grow in the spiritual life is a small parish prayer group. Such
associations have been widespread. Usually meeting at a designated time, weekly or less frequently, they engage in prayer,
Bible study, and the reading of devotional books. These books
might focus on methods of prayer or on developing ways of
meditation. Some learn from the writings of those proficient in
the spiritual life. Members of the group pray vocally and meditate silently in one another's company. They reinforce and
strengthen one another through corporate prayer, study, and
action.

A pitfall of such prayer group is that it can become ingrown,
leaving each person at the end of the session with a warm feeling of the nearness of God, but untouched by any impulse to
share God's love. When the focus of a spiritual group is on
developing power to live more effectively as religious persons,
intercession, which is so important a component, can lead them
to find ways of expressing their prayer in action. This helps to
maintain a balance between a subjectivity that could become
sentimental, and the objective reality that intercession represents.

Such groups may also become ingrown if they do not admit
new members. A kind of "coziness" can develop that shuts out
people who did not belong to the group when it first formed.
Prayer groups need to attract new people and should welcome
the opportunity of growth by dividing into two groups. This
would be a sign of their vitality and effectiveness. They exist,
not simply to nourish the spiritual life of an individual, but to
deepen the spiritual life of a parish. They need to meet at times
when people will be available, whether morning, afternoon, or

evening; on a weekday or at the weekend. The focus should be as varied as the needs. Some people will learn from exemplars who lived in the past and some need to know about contemporaries. Others want to become aware of dimensions for cultivating the life of prayer, such as the use of symbols or other images, the Ignatian method of picturing a biblical situation, or silent meditation on a verse of hymn or scripture. They could be introduced to the use of the Jesus Prayer. People are enriched by both study and practice of the different avenues into the spiritual life.[12]

Retreats are a familiar method for spiritual development in the Roman Catholic and Anglican traditions. The silent retreat has been found by many to be a way of relaxing, listening, becoming refreshed, and being strengthened. Many report that they mentally leave their cares when they enter the retreat center, and because of that conscious effort, are able to return home with a new perspective at the close of the retreat. The word "retreat" has never meant (even in military circles) to run away. It has meant a deliberate withdrawal to become refreshed, strengthened, and reoriented in order to regroup for the struggle. Life is a struggle, even at its best. Living as a religious person in a society that may present ethical conflicts causes stress. Deliberately going away from a situation in order to view life in the presence of God offers solutions for problems which had earlier seemed intractable.

A retreat does not depend for its effectiveness on the person who is leading it. The leader's talks may or may not be personally helpful. They are always few and usually brief. The opportunity for counseling with the retreat leader may be an important aspect for some retreatants. A primary factor is the retreat setting, which needs to be a simple but comfortable building, usually on spacious grounds, where each person has a separate room, and meals are quietly offered. Regular times of worship at morning, noon, and evening alternate with periods for quiet in one's room, the chapel, the grounds, or some comfortable reading corner. These surroundings somehow convey a pervasive sense of the presence of God. Retreatants find truth in the words of Isaiah: "In returning and rest you shall be saved; in quietness and trust shall be your strength" (Isa. 30:15).

Many have never participated in a silent retreat. They would feel uncomfortable with so little speech. Such people need to be prepared for the experience. Modifications of the classical pattern are already being practiced. Meals eaten without conversation may be accompanied by musical recordings as an alternative to the more usual reading from a carefully selected book that is meditative but not "heavy." Retreat talks may be followed by informal times of discussion and sharing for those who wish to do so. But the basic intent is to have ample time during which one's whole being is focused on listening to God and experiencing the presence of God, both alone and in a worshiping group.

Throughout the years, there are specified times when one can be educated for the spiritual life. Children can be prepared for participation in Sunday worship. They can learn from parents and teachers how to find spiritual meaning in hymns, prayer, scripture, and the liturgy of the Lord's Supper. When people are being prepared for baptism or confirmation they can be helped to review their spiritual life up to that point and understand that such development is a growing process that can become deepened during this preparatory time and will continue to deepen throughout life if they desire to cultivate the relationship with God.

The Roman Catholic and some Anglican churches have had liturgical services that, because of a specific focus, became a way of helping people deepen the spiritual life.[13] One such service is Benediction, a quiet liturgy of devotion designed to bring people into the Presence of Christ. The consecrated Host in a monstrance is carried in procession through the church and later returned to the aumbry, where the reserved Sacrament is customarily kept. The Rosary is a devotional practice to help people remember the birth, life, death, and resurrection of Jesus as they meditate on these events while touching each of a series of beads, praying at specific intervals the Hail Mary and the Our Father. Meditation on the Lord's Prayer, with a pause after each petition, is itself a framework for devotion that can enrich the unison use of the prayer during congregational worship.

The Stations of the Cross originated in the pilgrim path followed by thousands of believers along the streets of Old Jerusalem, where there are still markers at the fourteen places at which worshippers pause to meditate along the Way of the Cross, from the Place of Judgment to Golgotha. Today symbols of these stations are placed along the walls of a church or chapel. The art forms may be carved in wood, moulded in plaster, painted on canvas, or expressed through other media and in various styles. As the person pauses at each Station, words of scripture and prayer became the basis for meditation on the event. This devotional service can become one element in the liturgical life of a congregation during Lent, in preparation for Easter.[14]

Others have found spiritual enrichment through brief services of worship such as noonday prayers that focus on the Cross, and Compline, to commend life to God at night. As mentioned earlier, the imposition of ashes on Ash Wednesday and the words "Remember that you are dust and to dust you will return" are awesome reminders of personal mortality.

During Holy Week there is the service of Tenebrae, in which each of seven readings from the Psalms is concluded with the extinguishing of a candle in a seven-branched candlestick, until the church is left in total darkness. The Light of the World has been taken away for a time. In an alternative form of Tenebrae, gospel readings ranging from the account of the Last Supper to the sentencing of Jesus are read and at the conclusion the final light is extinguished.[15]

There are many methods for spiritual formation: some are individual, and some depend on the interaction of believing people. Some methods are conducive to spiritual growth because of the setting, people, or reading. Others draw their power from liturgies. Such variety demonstrates the fact that God meets people through many avenues. The more possibilities available, the more likely individuals will be to find a compatible path for growing in the spiritual life.

9. Interacting Elements in Spiritual Development

Spiritual development is directed toward wholeness of life. Such a goal involves an interaction of body, mind, and spirit within the self, in relation to God and to the vast created world.

Nurture and Education

The spiritual life is nurtured. Nurturing implies feeding, giving, and concern to meet needs. The plant that is fed grows, blooms, and bears fruit, thereby fulfilling its life. So too the person who is nurtured. A person requires food, a sustaining environment, and people who give love.

Nurture at first is an informal process, a natural mode of being; and particular nurture in the spiritual life is likewise experiential. A person who is spiritually aware manifests a gracious quality of life that declares this to be so. Those who come into proximity with such a person sense that by that other one they themselves are blessed. Every church has a few such people. Every family needs at least one. Many such people are apparent in the agencies and workplaces of every community.

Urban T. Holmes III has described spirituality as (1) a human capacity for relationship (2) that transcends sense phenomena; this relationship (3) is perceived by the subject as an expanded or heightened consciousness independent of the subject's efforts, (4) given substance in the historical setting, and (5) exhibits itself in creative action in the world.[1] Note in this definition that the spiritual person is described as aware of a relationship to the Transcendent (whom we name God) that develops in the particularity of time and place and is apparent in life.

Nurturing persons are capable of sharing with others their own life in God. This does not mean giving answers to unasked questions, but being available when another has a need to ask. "How do you manage to keep so cheerful?" you ask a friend, a note of amazement in your voice. "You convey to me a quiet strength I did not know could exist," you say to someone else. Your comment may elicit a verbally responsive witness to faith, or it may be that the other will simply receive it without any overt verbal response.

Persons become nurturers by living in caring communities. The family, whatever its form, is such a community, and spiritual life develops at least as much through the loving, forgiving, reconciling relationships there as it does through the concrete observances of prayer and other forms of celebration.

The church is a nurturing community, basically because believing people gather to worship God. The quality of their spirituality is evident in their approach and response to the service, especially the weekly Sunday liturgy. Persons also nurture one another through their lives together in church groups. This is evident to anyone who participates in a prayer group, but it can be equally evident in the way a congregation goes about its work; for example, the meetings of the governing board and parish committees.

Both the spirit and content of such meetings can either deepen or distract from the spiritual life of the members. One has only to read polls about why people say they do not participate in church life. Some are offended by the organizational life,[2] yet any social group, including a family, has organization, however informal. Clearly, the spirituality of church organizations has not appeared to be an influence for spiritual growth to many people.

The church also nurtures the spiritual life through the avenues it uses to obey the command of Jesus to proclaim the good news and to feed, clothe, and visit those in need. These are signs of belonging to the Kingdom of God. The *doing* is a form of nurturing because the presence of God is realized through engagement in activities that alleviate need or promote social justice.

Nurturing happens gradually. This is implied in the statement of the apostle Paul to feed milk before meat. The child is nurtured in small groups such as the family, or peers and teachers in church, through a gradual introduction to congregational worship, and by acts of service that can have meaning in the context of a child's experience. Older children, adolescents, and adults are nurtured in accordance with their various stages on life's way.

Education is different from nurture. To be sure, the educator is conscious of the nurturing process, but introduces deliberately structured experiences that include reflection on action. When the teacher tells a class the story of Toyohiko Kagawa or asks a member of the congregation to share her spiritual journey, the teacher will also ask the class, "Why do you think Kagawa was willing to spend a lifetime with the poor of Tokyo?" and "Why do you think our friend is able to share her life with you in this way?" The class begins the educational process of thinking in order to clarify the imaginal relationship with Kagawa and the affective relationship with another member of the congregation. It becomes evident as the class reasons from experiences that a disciplined life takes prayer, scripture and other devotional reading seriously, and that a life resulting from the interaction of these elements has produced the kind of person to whom the class has been introduced. Thus the learners now have the components for spiritual development, whether the quest is engaged in with a teacher (in class or through individual spiritual guidance), or in a group that has agreed to a segment of journeying together.

Next, the ways of prayer and the techniques for meditation

must be learned. Also, the study of scripture must include a serious attempt to understand the text before it can become a vehicle for hearing the word of God. Attempts to take short-cuts in either area indicate a lack of seriousness or an avoid-ance of spiritual discipline. The willingness to have or to be a spiritual mentor, guide, or friend (whatever the designation used) affirms the an interrelationship between teaching and learning. Structured experiences that translate spirituality into action encourage learners to convey the love of God in Christ to others.

Teaching is both giving and receiving. As in the nurturing process, at first the teacher's role is to give. The committed teacher recognizes that the long-range goal is slowly to with-draw so that the learner can become autonomous. The teacher as nurturer is less needed as the learner grows and develops the ability to discern other agencies for learning. A support group may teach as well as nurture, or a prayer group may open a knowledge of spiritual reading previously unsuspected. In time, the learner becomes teacher, sharing experience with others.

The teaching-learning process is also a process of holding and of letting go. The neophyte in the spiritual life may cling to the person or group that has been helpful in bringing the real-ity of god's presence. It gives a person pleasure to be needed, and one is tempted to cling to the role of provider. But in the ultimate sense, God alone is the provider. The spiritual guide, be this one person or a group, dares not keep another depen-dent, but finds true success in becoming participant in the joint process of life in God. This is the import of Clement of Alexan-dria's wise insight, written in the second century: that the hu-man teacher is the *paidogogus*, or guide, the slave who leads the child to the teacher. Christ is the teacher to whom the person is being led.[3] The teacher's work is not completed until the process of letting go has been accomplished. When the teacher can learn from the pupil, the task has been well done.

Spiritual Awareness Enlarges the Self

By referring to spiritual development as cultivation of the inner life, some people mistakenly view this as a way of nurturing an inner security. This is a misunderstanding, for such inwardness too easily becomes narcissistic. The spiritual life is not a matter of feeling that Jesus lives in the heart in some private relationship. God dwells within the human heart in order that we might be strengthened by God's spirit.

In the book *The Reasons of the Heart*, which will surely become a classic of modern spirituality, the author, John S. Dunne, views the spiritual life as a journey. On the road to God, he says, people begin with a solitude that in time becomes loneliness. Yet out of this loneliness comes the experience of God. One may not rest there. The awareness of God issues forth in the realization that God must be followed into the turmoil of human life. Dunne writes, after finding God in the solitude: "My life becomes a journey in time and God becomes my companion on the way, but I am left with an unfulfilled yearning for human companionship."[4] Only within the human circle is the spiritual life complete.

C. G. Jung made a contribution to the understanding of persons with his concepts of the introvert and the extrovert. The introverted person is most comfortable when alone or in a small group. Such a person can be content with hours of quiet, fulfills work tasks best when alone, and will probably have only a few close friends. The extrovert, on the contrary, is most fulfilled when part of a large group, studies and works best in the midst of the comforting sounds of activity, likes to join groups, and participates in community and family enterprises.

The spiritual life will develop differently for each of these psychological types.[5] Some can spend hours in solitary reading, prayer, and meditation. Even in the worship of the congregation, they feel drawn apart into their private experience. The words of hymns speak personally, but introverts may not be moved by the full sound of a singing congregation. During

Communion, they may feel an intimate association with God, but are less aware of the others with whom they are gathered around the Table. They may seek a spiritual guide, but are less likely to accept an invitation to participate in a prayer group. They may have some difficulty in carrying this relationship to God into works that will take them into any large social arena or require becoming involved in advocacy situations. Their spiritual discipline lies in relating the personal experience of God to the need for sharing and witnessing.

The hermit is the prototype of the introverted person. People seek the hermit in order to hear words of spiritual wisdom and experience brief proximity to a holy person. Thomas Merton was such a person, yet at the same time something extroverted in his personality always urged him to seek the company of others, whether at home or abroad, to share experiences of the disciplined spiritual life.

The wholly extroverted person evidences the spiritual life in another way. This person becomes uncomfortable during long hours spent alone. The yearning to be with others becomes an inhibiting factor in spiritual growth. Such a person needs briefer times of quiet devotion, spaced more widely through the day and week. Extroverted persons come alive in the large congregation. They are spiritually fed by being surrounded with other persons, lifting up their voices in hymns of praise and joining in unison prayer. Extroverts are likely to feel exalted by the proximity of others to share the bread and cup, they pass the peace with warmth, embracing as they say "The peace of the Lord be with you." Prayer groups assist in their development. Their spiritual life is fulfilled as they battle for righteousness' sake and spend their lives in efforts to bring the peace of God to a striving and strife-torn humanity.

Imagine what the world would be like without *both* kinds of people! How could God's work be accomplished if there were not the quiet ones who invite others to withdraw and who find strength in solitude? How could God's work be done if there were not people who felt called to accomplish the mission in a wider sphere? In the classical monastic communities, the introverts become attached to the Carthusians, Cistercians, and Carmelites; the extroverts to the Franciscans, servants of the poor; to the Augustinians, the preachers; and to the Dominicans, the teachers. The first of the Western orders, the Benedictines, was established in order to practice a balanced life of work, prayer, and study.

Both kinds of people will be living in a given community. Parish leaders need to be aware of this factor in the work they ask of people, and the opportunities offered for developing the spiritual life.

The spiritually aware person feels at one with the created world. Such a person does not believe that creation in the image of God gives human beings the right to use the earth and other creatures for their own gain and pleasure, but realizes that their own creation as humans is a special mandate from God to evidence the Holy Spirit in every part of creation that their lives touch. In turn, God's Spirit, alive in all creation, will empower their lives. The Holy Spirit is not grasped but is given.

This is not nature mysticism, and does not rest on the inward response generated by the human relationship to the world. Rather, such spiritual awareness eventuates in a dynamic activity through which people recognize a responsibility before God to find their place within the order of the universe. Through relationship to God, people can understand how other parts of creation are related to the Creator. Simplicity of life arises out of this kind of understanding. The nurturing of earth, through which its resources are renewed rather than dissipated, is an evidence of spirituality. The sense of the Transcendent is developed by such world-awareness, because the understanding of God does not become bound to the personal relationship to God. The holiness of God, which has always been a symbol for Transcendence, is, biblically speaking, an ethical holiness. The *mysterium tremendum*, of which Rudolf Otto speaks in his classical study, *The Idea of the Holy*, is so far beyond any conceptualization by humans that in the Divine Presence they feel

only an unworthiness. This is why people have offered the
firstfruits of the land to God, recognizing that only through
sun, soil, air, and water—which they can conserve but not create
—did they have the most basic sustenance for life. This recognition is basic to the spiritual life.

Spiritual development is real when a person is driven beyond
immediate personal concerns to a yearning that God's intention shall be made manifest in all human life, and that peace
might come upon earth. Even as the angels' song declared
peace among people of goodwill, so the transformation of the
human will to peace must be the basis for beating swords into
plowshares. We view the awful devastation in countries around
the world while sitting comfortably in the living room watching
from the safe distance of the television screen. How can we
nibble snacks while we watch starvation? Yet we do, every evening.

This sign of the spiritual life is directly connected with the
concern for the created world. The devastation of land and
people in the name of warring ideologies, each of which pro-
fesses to be intent only on bringing a better life to the surviving
inhabitants, is part of the human profanation of earth. Christ is
present in a war-torn land: the Cross is visible in the marks of
suffering on every human body. The Presence of God is manifested differently where sin and suffering are so egregiously
present than it is in the situations of the safe ones who watch,
and wait, and hope, but cannot decide what to do.

The yearning for peace is part of a yearning for the safety of
the human race whom God created and for whom Christ was
content to die. A redeemed humanity seems so far from reality
that some by losing hope have also lost all faith. The theological philosopher Richard L. Rubenstein has never accepted the
idea that after the Holocaust, the Jews could still regard themselves as a "chosen" people. The irony of the "chosenness" is
too much for him to accept.[6]

The Figure on the Cross, Christ crucified, is a paradigm of
what chosenness can mean. That is why Christian spirituality is

deeply bound up with walking the way of the Cross. As Passover celebrates the consummation of God's purpose, so also does Easter. The spiritual life is an Easter faith. After that event, disciples became apostles. Everyone needs to know a point in life at which she or he turned from discipleship to the apostolate. For the ex-fishermen, who, after the crucifixion, returned to their trade on Lake Galilee, this meant responding to the Figure on the shore. The words spoken during their early days together in Galilee were repeated: "Follow me." The book The Acts of the Apostles gives some glimpses into what that meant.

Spiritual development has an ecumenical dimension and even a global dimension, as common elements have enriched the lives of seekers from Christian, Jewish, Muslim, Hindu, and Buddhist traditions. Within the Christian world, until recently, Western forms of spirituality denoted the parameters of spiritual development. In the wisdom of God, revelation has been given to all the peoples of earth. The Christian churches in Asian and African countries long retained evidences of their spiritual heritage and sought to become incorporated into a Western tradition. Only recently have these churches been encouraged to develop their own forms of spirituality. As a minority group within a non-Christian nation, Christians have distinctive boundaries within their national culture. As they feel more accepted as Christians they will feel more confident to develop an indigenous Christian spirituality.

Among Western Christians, the sharing of spiritual traditions has accelerated in recent years. One notices few differences of style or terminology in reading Roman Catholic or Protestant writers. Catholic retreat centers have often become favored gathering places for Protestant conferences. Would that Protestants might also accept the guidance of Catholic retreat leaders and develop the practice of spiritual retreats.

The rich treasury of Eastern Christian spirituality is beginning to enter the consciousness of Western Christians. At the Vancouver Assembly of the World Council of Churches in

1983, for example, a service of Sharing the Bread was led by Metropolitan Chrysostomos of the Ecumenical Patriarchate in Constantinople. Also, elements from Orthodox worship were incorporated into the Sunday Eucharist, which used the "Lima" Liturgy, so called because it was developed by an ecumenical liturgical study group that met at Lima, Peru, in 1982. Mutual sharing in the development of the spiritual life is probably more a reality than is ecumenical understanding in theology or liturgics. The shared task of biblical interpretation is one factor in this process of cross-fertilization.

The Spirituality of Everyday Life

A spiritual life formed through an awareness of being part of the whole created world, which yearns for the peaceful upbuilding of human life on all the earth and has absorbed spiritual dimensions from around the world, brings a unique perspective to the spirituality of everyday life. The term "everyday" sounds mundane. One thinks of the daily round of activities: such tasks as child rearing, homemaking, earning a living, church and community service. But these are the activities in which God is made known. Donald G. Bloesch, in *The Crisis of Piety*, is critical of the kind of "Jesus piety" that leads people to neglect the realization that devotion means both adoration and obedience. This spirituality is grounded in Paul's affirmation about justification: that while we were still sinners, Christ died for us.[7] Bloesch believes that a recovery of the spiritual life can come only when people are willing to take upon themselves the spiritual disciplines of prayer, study, fasting, abstinence, and simplicity, accepting a deliberate structure for Sunday observance and participation in the Lord's Supper. He is critical of some forms of evangelical piety that have neglected the factors of repentance and obedience, resting on the assurance of personal salvation.

Everyday life is not a confined experience, untouched by the surrounding world. Attempts to practice a completely interiorized faith would be a negation of biblical spirituality. While elements in spiritual development are common to all generations, a new note has crept into books written since 1940. One person who became uneasy with attempts to adapt Christianity to the patterns of society was Dietrich Bonhoeffer. People quote phrases such as "religionless Christianity" and Christianity in a "world come of age." Bonhoeffer also spoke of *deus ex machina,* by which he meant the expectation that God would patch things up some day, regardless of how humans acted to bring about disaster. Bonhoeffer saw that the comfortable pieties which had up to that point guided spiritual development were no longer certain. "Radical Christianity" in a literal sense was getting to the roots of the spiritual life. This meant withdrawing from the world, sustained by belonging to a small committed community, venturing forth to do battle in God's name against the powers of Satan, armored in the might of shared prayer and other forms of spiritual discipline. He knew himself to be living in the kind of world in which Paul lived when speaking of putting on the whole armor of God. Bonhoeffer did not bolster up his view of the church by reading statistics about church membership and church attendance, nor by studying manuals on effective church growth. His definitive statement, a classic of twentieth-century spirituality, is *Life Together.*[8] This book describes the discipline of a committed community of pastors who, with prescient vision born of faith, anticipated the massive evil that was to come upon their nation. A different kind of social order required a different form of spiritual development.

Twentieth-century writers on spirituality have pointed to the factor of "desacralization," by which they mean that there is no sense of the Sacred or the Transcendent in human society. Everything and everyone is treated as temporal, touchable, or obtainable. Secularization was a popular term in the 1960s, and carried a positive connotation.[9] One did not have to go as far as the "death-of-God" theologians to recognize that in Western cultures religion was considered marginal. This fact was justified by referring to a covenant community, or a people who are called; "the remnant" or a "committed minority." As Bonhoeffer had earlier perceived, Christianity occupied a place similar to that which it had during its first centuries in the Roman Empire, except that today Christians are sometimes deceived about their position because of the rich deposit of residual Christianity continuing from past centuries.

The affirmation of secularity that was of such concern to writers through the 1960s receded, to be followed by an emphasis on interiority. This was epitomized by the popularity with believers and nonbelievers alike of Yoga exercises, Zen meditation, and Transcendental Meditation. The long tradition of Christian spirituality was neglected, partly because people were ignorant of its existence. The role of the guru was accepted but that of a spiritual director was nearly unknown.

The emphasis on the spiritual life has continued, but today Christian forms of spiritual development are recognized and encouraged. The task is to develop spiritual disciplines to meet the needs of life in a secular society. This requires spiritual regimens in a culture where Sunday is little different from other days, except that some people attend church, while others do so on Saturday; Christmas and Easter develop such secular interpretations that the church has difficulty teaching its own people the true meaning, and life is so filled with activities that devotional manuals suggest moments of prayer while the traffic light is red.

The everyday practice of spirituality brings a person constantly into the agonizing realization of the ambiguity in which a Christian lives. We want love and justice in our personal lives and in ever-widening circles of relationships, yet we must rest content with only the smallest glimpses of what this can mean. It is no longer possible to cultivate only a neighborhood mentality in the global awareness of twentieth-century life; hence the spiritual life becomes filled with images from the national and world scene. This wider reference brings a deep sense of one's humanness and can open a person to the transcendent power of God. There is no longer the illusion that humans can create a new world.

The Balance Between the Transcendent and the Immanent

In addition to a balance between the personal and the global, or the spiritual and the secular, there is a need for balance between awareness of the transcendent nature of God and the immanent presence of God. Eugene B. Borowitz analyzes this in a perceptive article in which he points out the shortcomings of the rational approach to religion for apprehending the Transcendent.[10] Writing from a Jewish perspective, he points out that those in the liberal, or Reform, tradition who have sought the path of spirituality through rational conceptualization, have added an emotional component, or relied on the experience of the community. They have developed an ethical component by doing good works and helping individuals, or have concentrated on self-awareness (the psychological approach). Finally they have taken the mystical path to the Transcendent Other.

Borowitz states five paradoxes with which contemporary religious people must live. The wholly Other is beyond thought and speech, so although our usual approach is verbal, we can most clearly become aware of God on a preverbal level. Since humans are symbol-makers, vital rites and symbols are needed in order to nurture the approach to God, but we have neglected developing the symbolic life. Constancy, persistence, and regularity are necessary in order to develop the relationship to God, but we prefer to believe that the spiritual life comes spontaneously. People desire an experience of inner peace, but will not accept the fact that this peace is attained only through the struggle of a disciplined spirituality. We need to make spirituality an integrating factor in life, yet find that life is filled with surprises that make integration difficult.[11]

Christians have frequently felt a conflict between the comfortableness of a personal relationship to God and the formality

of a church service. This could be a reason for the finding of
the poll-takers that many people feel they can worship God
better alone than in church.[12] Among Protestants, particularly,
there has been a serious lack of realization that objective and
subjective factors together in worship are the only way to a
fully integrated relationship with God. Some people may derive from a formal liturgy a fearsome mental image of God as a
Judge who will bring the world to an end and visit eternal
wrath upon the human race. Such a picture ignores the fact
that biblical people prayed for the consummation of God's
Kingdom and yearned for the time when they would enjoy the
fruits of redemption: a new heaven and a new earth.

The distance between God and people is the difference between the Creator and the creature, the initiator and the re-
sponder—that is, the difference between the Divine and the
human. God alone could and did bridge the gap: to the Jews
through Law and Covenant; to the Christians through Jesus
Christ.

The full power of the spiritual life can only be known when
the transcendent quality of God is appreciated. Humans express this awareness of the holy in symbolic forms such as liturgies, church buildings, and hymns. It is expressed in Isaiah
16:30: "Holy, Holy, Holy is the Lord of hosts. The whole earth
is full of his glory," and similarly in The Revelation to John 4:8.
Meditation on scripture and hymnody as well as on the writings
of the mystics communicates this awareness.

The complement to this insight is the realization that the
Transcendent One is also the personal Thou who meets the
human I. Such practices as individual prayer and spiritual reading meet this need. So does the intimacy of a small group, or an
informal liturgy. People need memories of times when each of
these devotional forms was a way of practicing the presence of
God. In this ecumenical time, it would be well for people deliberately to seek opportunities for worship with those who
have methods with which one is unaccustomed. In addition,
every congregation needs to cultivate both forms of approach

to God in order to help people develop a balanced spiritual life.[13]

Spirituality and the Cross

The Cross is central to Western Christian spirituality. Although the Eastern church usually depicts, in ikon and mosaic, Christ in glory, and although this is the theme of the great tapestry that forms the background for the altar in the present Coventry Cathedral, England, the Cross has more often been set above altar, pulpit, or Table. There are many forms: an empty Cross; a crucifix with twisted body; or a serenely regal figure. In each generation one form of the Cross has fitted more nearly the situation of the people than did another form. Likewise, many great artists of the Western cultures have made the crucifixion a focal point for their canvasses. There can be either a dramatic richness or an awesome simplicity in the way an artist interprets the scene. Protestants have developed hymnody around the theme of the Cross, frequently in words that affirmed the redemption in Christ and assured the believer of salvation.

So deep is the suffering human beings endure, and so manifold its forms, that it is no wonder Jesus crucified becomes a paradigm for mortal existence. Lent is an older observance than Advent, and the drama of Holy Week has been replayed and relived since the earliest Christian centuries. In their hour of trial, believers have identified with Jesus and felt that here was one who understood their need. They have believed that they were affirming their commitment to him when they accepted their suffering with patience. They hear the words in 1 Peter, addressed to Christians in a time of testing: "For to this you have been called, because Christ also suffered for you, leaving you an example, that you should follow in his steps" (1 Pet. 2:21).

The Rosary, developed during the late Middle Ages, concentrates in part on the seven sorrowful mysteries (that is, the trial and suffering of Christ), and the Stations of the Cross are a liturgy through which people can participate in the path to Calvary. The liturgy of the Lord's Supper, in some traditions more than others, has emphasized participation in the death of Christ. The Passion narrative is the longest section in each gospel.

But there is another side. Among those who went on the road to Calvary were the crucifiers, and we find ourselves among them. This is part of the discipline for the spiritual life: to recognize whatever in ourselves prevents full commitment to Christ, whatever in ourselves is angered by the sight of someone like Jesus, who so fully accepts the will of God and trusts in the eventual completion of God's purpose.

The acceptance of the Cross is necessary, for without Good Friday there can be no Easter. Christian faith is an Easter faith. The proclamation is anticipated in Isaac Watts' Passion hymn "When I Survey the Wondrous Cross." The hymn concludes: "Were the whole realm of nature mine, / That were an off'ring far too small; / Love so amazing, so divine, / Demands my soul, my life, my all." Dazzling phrases like "realm of nature," " . . . love so amazing, so divine," indicate that the writer is not really standing at Golgotha on Good Friday. He has already seen the shining light of the Resurrection.

An Easter faith tells the believer that Christ is always present—to the individual, the church, and the world. Spiritual disciplines, including whatever events life brings unasked, are positive enrichment for the life in God because they are ways through which God acts. One does not practice prayer to an absent God, or know the Transcendent One through meditation for self-awareness. A worship service would be for a non-believer a performance where fine music, stimulating preaching, and beautiful liturgical forms would bring aesthetic satisfaction. Without faith, such practices bring intellectual, aesthetic, or emotional reinforcement to a discipline of self-help. The believer knows another Reality.

The Easter appearances of the Risen Lord were limited; but

the Easter faith continued through the mandate to preach and teach. The experience at Pentecost occasioned a new kind of spirituality, continually in process of renewal. What does it mean to live in the Spirit? How is the Holy Spirit manifested in the world? One dare not attempt to determine this, for the purposes of God are beyond human limitations. Christians live in the age of the Spirit: not because Pentecost is an annual season of the Christian year, but because it is that extended time between Resurrection and return, between signs of promise and fulfillment, between the inauguration of the rule of God and its completion.

This can indeed be cause for ecstasy even in a suffering and tragically sinful world.

The spiritual life is nurtured and taught to each individual who lives in the context of a believing community. This spirituality has both a personal and a communal dimension. It begins with God's offer of faith that awaits human acceptance. The effects of such commitment spread in concentric circles into the life of church, community, nation, and world. The spiritual life requires an openness to God: to accept the offer of that "closer walk," to be sensitive to silence, to be willing to learn from those who have walked longer and more faithfully in the Way. There is no more assured path for living confidently, dying hopefully, and, during the interval between, sharing Christ's life with others along the pilgrim road.

Notes

Chapter 1: Hearts That Are Restless

1. Kenneth A. Briggs, "Faith Inspires These Actors' Efforts," *New York Times*, 22 August 1982, p. 5.
2. Joshua Loth Liebman, *Peace of Mind* (New York: Simon and Schuster, 1946); Fulton J. Sheen, *Peace of Soul* (New York: McGraw-Hill, 1949); Norman Vincent Peale, *The Power of Positive Thinking* (Englewood Cliffs, N.J.: Prentice-Hall, 1952).
3. Jessie Orton Jones, *Secrets* (New York: Viking, 1945).
4. This need is addressed in Thomas Harris, *I'm OK—You're OK* (New York: Harper & Row, 1967).
5. Jonathan Schell, *Fate of the Earth* (New York: Knopf, 1982).
6. Hence the popularity of a book addressed to this religious issue: Harold S. Kushner, *When Bad Things Happen to Good People* (New York: Shocken, 1981).
7. Erik Erikson, "Identity and the Life Cycle," *Psychological Issues* 1, no. 1 (1959): 86.
8. Jerome S. Bruner, *Toward a Theory of Instruction* (Cambridge: Harvard University Press, 1966), p. 44.
9. Ibid., p. 64.
10. Teilhard de Chardin, *The Divine Milieu: An Essay on the Interior Life* (New York: Harper & Row, 1960).
11. Martin Buber, *I and Thou*, trans. and ed. Walter Kauffman (New York: Scribner's, 1970).
12. St. Meinrad School of Theology, St. Meinrad, Ind., *Learning to Pray Alone: A Study and Program to Aid Diocesan Candidates for Priesthood.* Project funded by the Lilly Foundation, Inc. (Indianapolis: 1979).

Chapter 2: The Process of Spiritual Growth

1. R. M. French, trans. *The Way of a Pilgrim* and *The Pilgrim Continues His Way* (New York: Harper & Row, 1954).
2. Julian of Norwich, *Showings* (New York: Paulist, 1978).
3. *The Little Flowers of St. Francis*, trans. Raphael Brown (New York: Doubleday, 1971).
4. E. Glenn Hinson, ed., *The Journal of George Fox*, Doubleday Devotional Classics, vol. 2 (New York: Doubleday, 1978).
5. Francis de Sales, *Introduction to the Devout Life* (New York: Harper & Row, 1952).

6. *Spiritual Letters: Selections from Fenelon,* no. 2 (Boston: Roberts Bros., 1890).
7. Thomas Kelly, *A Testament of Devotion,* ed. E. Glenn Hinson, Doubleday Devotional Classics, vol. 3 (1978).
8. Charles M. Magsam, *The Experience of God: Outlines for a Contemporary Spirituality* (Maryknoll: Orbis, 1975), p. 221.
9. Buber, *I and Thou.*
10. Louis J. Puhl, trans., *The Spiritual Exercises of St. Ignatius Loyola* (Westminster, Md.: Newman Press, 1951).

Chapter 3: Tracing the Spiritual Way

1. Urban T. Holmes, *A History of Christian Spirituality: An Analytic Introduction* (New York: Seabury, 1981), p. 4. This book is a masterly, brief presentation of people and their ideas, in both the Eastern and Western branches of the church. A fuller basic source is Louis Bouyer et al., *A History of Christian Spirituality* in 3 volumes (New York, Seabury, 1982).
2. Clement of Alexandria, *Christ the Educator,* trans. Francis P. Wood, The Fathers of the Church Series, vol. 23 (Washington, D.C.: Catholic University Press, 1954), p. 4.
3. Gregory of Nyssa, *The Life of Moses,* Classics of Western Spirituality (New York: Paulist Press, 1978), p. 113.
4. Augustine, *Confessions,* trans. Vernon J. Bourke, The Fathers of The Church Series, vol. 21 (Washington, D.C.: Catholic University Press, 1953), p. 185.
5. Holmes, *A History of Christian Spirituality,* p. 48.
6. Bernard of Clairvaux, *Treatises II,* The Works of Bernard of Clairvaux (Cistercian Publications, Consortium Press, 1974), p. 105.
7. James Walsh, ed., *The Cloud of Unknowing,* Classics of Western Spirituality (New York: Paulist, 1981), pp. 120–121.
8. *The Collected Works of St. Teresa of Avila,* trans. Kieran Kavanaugh and Otilio Rodriguez (Washington, D.C.: ICS Publications, 1976), 1:151.
9. E. Glenn Hinson, ed., *The Journal of George Fox,* p. 402.
10. The Doubleday Devotional Classics Series; "Classics of Western Spirituality," Paulist Press. Also complete editions of the works of individual persons, such as the works of Bernard of Clairvaux, now being prepared by Cistercian Publications, and the Collected Works of Teresa of Avila, published by the Institute of Carmelite Studies.

Chapter 4: Learning from One Another

1. Gershom Scholem is the leading authority on this subject. *Kabbalah,* New American Library (1974; reprint ed., New York: Meridian Books, 1978).
2. *Your Word Is Fire: The Hasidic Masters on Contemplative Prayer,* ed. and trans. Arthur Green and Barry W. Holtz (New York: Paulist, 1977), p. 61. The Shekinah or Divine Presence is feminine in gender.
3. Another expression of Hasidic faith is illustrated through stories of the rabbis. See, for example, Arthur J. Band, ed., in *The Tales of Nahman of Bratslavtr,* Classics of Western Spirituality (New York: Paulist, 1978).
4. Martin Buber, *I and Thou,* p. 197.

5. Abraham Joshua Heschel, *The Quest for God* (1954; reprint, New York: Crossroad, 1982), p. 10.
6. Kenneth Cragg, *The Wisdom of the Sufis* (New York: New Directions, 1976), p. 37.
7. Ibid., p. 81.
8. Jean Marie Dechanet, *Christian Yoga* (New York: Harper & Row, 1960), or *Yoga and God, An Introduction to Christian Yoga* (St. Meinrad, Ind.: Abbey Press, 1975).
9. Beatrice Lane Suzuki, *Mahayana Buddhism* (1959; reprint, New York: Macmillan, 1969), p. 127.
10. Aelrad Graham, *Zen Catholicism* (New York: Harcourt Brace, 1963).
11. John S. Mbiti, *The Prayers of African Religion* (Maryknoll, N.Y.: Orbis, 1975), p. 151.
12. Una Kroll, *The Healing Potential of Transcendental Meditation* (Atlanta: John Knox, 1974). A brief introduction is Anthony Campbell, *TM and the Nature of Enlightenment* (New York: Harper & Row, 1975).
13. Thomas Merton, *Mystics and Zen Masters* (New York: Farrar, Straus and Giroux, 1961), p. x.

Chapter 5: *Conflict and Spiritual Growth*

1. Martin Luther, *A Brief Explanation of the Creed* (Philadelphia; Holman), 2:368.
2. Søren Kierkegaard, *Purity of Heart Is to Will One Thing*, trans. Douglas Steere (New York: Harper & Row, 1938), p. 31.
3. Proper II, the Sunday closest to July 20. *The Book of Common Prayer* (New York: Seabury, 1977), p. 231.
4. Louis Schneider and Sanford M. Dornbusch, *Popular Religion: Inspirational Books in America* (Chicago: University of Chicago Press, 1950).
5. Gerald G. May, *Care of Mind, Care of Spirit: Psychiatric Dimensions of Spiritual Direction* (San Francisco: Harper & Row, 1982), p. 24.

Chapter 6: *Roots of Spirituality*

1. This question has been addressed profoundly and simply by Rabbi Harold S. Kushner, *When Bad Things Happen to Good People* (New York: Schocken, 1981).
2. C. G. Jung, *Modern Man in Search of a Soul* (New York: Harcourt Brace, 1953).
3. Ann Belford Ulanov, *Psychology and Religion* and *Religion and the Unconscious* (Philadelphia: Westminster, 1975).
4. Morton F. Kelsey, *Dreams: A Way to Listen to God* (New York: Paulist, 1978). Also John A. Sanford, *Dreams: God's Forgotten Language* (New York: Crossroad, 1982).
5. Abraham Maslow, *Religion, Values and Peak Experiences* (Columbus: Ohio State University Press, 1964).
6. Morton T. Kelsey, *The Christian and the Supernatural* (Minneapolis: Augsburg, 1976).
7. For more on this subject, see my *Christian Child Development* (San Francisco: Harper & Row, 1979).

186 / Notes

8. See Ira Progoff, *A Journal Workshop* (New York: Dialogue House Library, 1975).
9. Mircea Eliade, *Myth and Reality,* (New York: Harper & Row, 1963).

Chapter 7: Nurture in Spirituality

1. James Fowler, *Stages of Faith: A Psychology of Human Development and the Quest for Meaning* (San Francisco: Harper & Row, 1981), p. xiii.
2. Erik H. Erikson, "Identity and the Life Cycle," *Psychological Issues* 1, no. 1 (1959): 61–62.
3. Jean Piaget, *Six Psychological Studies* (New York: Vintage, 1967), pp. 3 f.
4. For Fowler this is the mythic-literal stage.
5. David Elkind, *The Child's Reality* (New York: Halstead, 1978), pt. 2.
6. Andre Godin, "Parental Images and the Divine Paternity," *Lumen Vitae* 19 (1964): 253 f.
7. Robert Williams, "A Theory of God-Concept Readiness from the Piagetian Theories of Child Artificialism and the Origin of Religious Feeling in Children," *Religious Education* 62, no. 1 (1971): 62 f.
8. Edward Robinson, *The Original Vision: A Study of the Religious Experience of Childhood* (New York: Seabury, 1973). From the introduction to the American edition, pp. x–xi.
9. Lewis J. Sherrill, *The Struggle of the Soul* (New York: Macmillan, 1951).
10. "Everybody Rides the Carousel," a film view of life stages with reference to the developmental theories of Erik H. Erikson.
11. For Fowler this is the stage of synthetic-conventional faith, which must bring a coherence in faith, usually accomplished through interaction of the various factors in the total environment of the adolescent. He notes that many adults remain in this stage. While a person may indeed form a personal faith, this may become so rigidly held as to preclude modification when changes seem indicated in the church environment (Fowler, *Stages of Faith*, pp. 172–73).
12. Note Roman Catholic documents on the rite of adult Christian initiation. Also, *Confirmation Re-Examined,* ed. Kendig Brubaker Cully (Wilton, Conn.: Morehouse-Barlow, 1982).
13. Daniel J. Levinson, *The Seasons of a Man's Life* (New York: Ballantine Books, 1978). Parallel work is now being done on the developmental stages of women. So also *Faith Development in the Adult Life Cyle,* ed. Kenneth Stokes (New York: Sadlier, 1982).
14. In Fowler's typology, the young adult is in stage 4, Individuative-Reflexive Faith, arising from an ability to look critically at issues. Stage 5, Conjunctive Faith, if it develops, belongs to midlife and involves the ability to recognize the disjunctive situations of life. These people can accept others whose beliefs differ, respond to social need, and appreciate ritual. Stage 6, Universalizing Faith, carries a person beyond the bounds of a specific faith-community into an awareness of an essential unity among forms of faith.
15. The interaction of spiritual factors with psychological development is the basis for Evelyn Eaton Whitehead and James D. Whitehead, *Christian Life Patterns: The Psychological Challenges and Religious Invitations of Adult Life* (New York: Doubleday, 1982).

16. The roles of child, family, and church in religious development are considered in my *Christian Child Development* (San Francisco: Harper & Row, 1979).
17. This is called the "Quem Quaeritis" strophe and may be found in collections of English drama or of religious drama.

Chapter 8: Methods for Spiritual Development

1. Introductions to Transcendental Meditation for children are beginning to appear. From the Christian perspective, a recent book is Theresa O'Callaghan Scheihing with Louis M. Savary, *Our Treasured Heritage: Teaching Christian Meditation to Children* (New York: Paulist, 1982).
2. Preparation for meditation is described in Elizabeth O'Connor, *Search for Silence* (Waco; Tex.: Word, 1972), pt. 2.
3. Gerald G. May, *Care of Mind, Care of Spirit: Psychiatric Dimensions of Spiritual Direction* (San Francisco: Harper & Row, 1982), p. 55.
4. Abraham Joshua Heschel, *Quest for God: Studies in Prayer and Symbolism* (1954; reprint, New York: Crossroad, 1983).
5. Ibid., pp. 77–78.
6. Ibid., p. 97.
7. Ann and Barry Ulanov, *Primary Speech: A Psychology of Prayer* (Atlanta: John Knox Press, 1982), p. 1.
8. Ibid., pp. 96–97.
9. James C. Fenhagen, *More Than Wanderers* (New York: Seabury, 1978), p. 36.
10. Ibid., p. 95. For more books in this area see Tilden Edwards, *Spiritual Friend: Reclaiming the Gift of Spiritual Direction* (New York: Paulist, 1980); Kenneth Leech, *Soul Friend: The Practice of Spiritual Direction* (San Francisco: Harper & Row, 1977); Alan W. Jones, *Exploring Spiritual Direction: An Essay on Christian Friendship* (New York: Seabury, 1982); Francis W. Vanderwall, *Spiritual Direction: An Invitation to Abundant Life* (New York: Paulist, 1982); William A. Barry and William A. Connolly, *The Practice of Spiritual Direction* (New York: Seabury, 1982); Jesse N. Trotter, *Christian Wholeness: Spiritual Direction for Today* (Wilton, Conn.: Morehouse-Barlow, 1982). See also J. Neufelder and M. Coelho, eds., *Writings on Spiritual Direction* (New York: Seabury, 1982).
11. Gerald G. May writes, "It is my belief that the primary task of spiritual directors is to encourage within themselves this moment-by-moment attention toward God as frequently as possible during spiritual direction sessions. . . . It helps to begin the session with quiet prayer and with a silent plea for grace to help one truly be a channel of God's truth and love for the other person. During the session itself, it is usually necessary to keep reorienting oneself toward God" (May, *Care of Mind, Care of Spirit,* p. 95).
12. Helpful books would be Thomas Merton, *Contemplative Prayer* (New York: Herder and Herder, 1969), and Morton T. Kelsey, *The Other Side of Silence: A Guide to Christian Meditation* (New York: Paulist, 1976).
13. See *The Book of Common Prayer* (New York: Seabury, 1977), and *The Book of Occasional Services* (New York: The Church Hymnal Corporation, 1979).

14. A variety of liturgies is described in John Macquarrie, *Paths in Spirituality* (New York: Harper & Row, 1972), and John H. Westerhoff III and John D. Eusden, *The Spiritual Life: Learning East and West* (New York: Seabury, 1982).

15. For this and other liturgies see also *From Ashes to Fire: Services of Worship for the Seasons of Lent and Easter* (Nashville: Abingdon, 1979); *Stations of the Cross for Children* (New York: Paulist); and Diane Abajian, *Praying and Doing the Stations of the Cross with Children* (Mystic, Conn.: Twenty-Third Publications). For adults: Jim Nisbet, *An Illustrated Stations of the Cross: The Devotion and Its History* (Mystic, Conn.: Twenty-Third Publications).

Chapter 9: Interacting Elements in Spiritual Development

1. Urban T. Holmes, *Spirituality for Ministry* (San Francisco: Harper & Row, 1982), p. 12. Some of the areas considered are poverty, sexuality, worship, the unconscious, parish piety, and spiritual companionship. The book is addressed to pastors and parishioners.

2. *A Summary of Qualitative Research of the Unchurched* (New York: Religion in American Life, n.d.), p. 40.

3. *Basic Writings in Christian Education*, ed. Kendig Brubaker Cully (Philadelphia: Westminster, 1960); Clement of Alexandria, *Christ the Educator*, trans. Francis P. Wood, The Fathers of the Church Series, vol. 23 (Washington, D.C.: Catholic University Press, 1954), pp. 17 f.

4. John S. Dunne, *The Reasons of the Heart: A Journey into Solitude and Back Again into the Human Circle* (New York: Macmillan, 1978), p. 136.

5. This insight from Jung was explicated by Sr. Elaine Prevalet, Sisters of Loretto, Loretto, Kentucky, who heads the retreat center there, in an address at Lexington (Ky.) Theological Seminary, March 17, 1983.

6. Richard Rubenstein, *After Auschwitz: Essays in Contemporary Judaism* (Indianapolis: Bobbs-Merrill, 1966).

7. Donald G. Bloesch, *The Crisis of Piety* (Grand Rapids: Eerdmans, 1968), p. 53.

8. Dietrich Bonhoeffer, *Life Together* (New York: Harper & Row, 1954).

9. Some books in this area are: Harvey Cox, *The Secular City: Secularization and Urbanization in Theological Perspective* (New York: Macmillan, 1965); Douglas A. Rhymes, *Prayer in the Secular City* (London: Lutterworth, 1967) and *Spirituality in the Secular City* (London: Lutterworth, 1967); *Spirituality in the Secular City*, eds. Christian Doquoc and Claude Geffre, *Concilium*, vol. 19 (New York: Paulist 1966); Henry Rack, *Twentieth-Century Spirituality* (London: Epworth, 1969).

10. Eugene B. Borowitz, "Beyond Immanence," *Religious Education* 75, no. 4 (July–August 1980): 387 f.

11. Ibid.

12. *A Summary of Qualitative Research of the Unchurched*, p. 16.

13. Henri J. M. Nouwen, *Reaching Out: The Three Movements of Spiritual Life* (New York: Doubleday, 1975), speaks to the rhythms of the spiritual life.

Index

Wesley, John, 30, 42, 62, 115
Wesleyans, 40
Westerhoff, John H. III, 188
Whitehead, Evelyn Eaton, 186
Whitehead, James D., 186
Williams College, 90
Williams, Robert, 186
Woolman, John, 61, 115

work, 3, 5
World Council of Churches, 175

Xavier, Francis, 72

Yoga, 73, 177

Zen, 74 f., 177